D0049293

CHOPIN

A biography, with a survey of
books, editions and recordings

THE CONCERTGOER'S COMPANIONS
SERIES EDITOR ALEC HYATT KING

BACH by Alec Robertson
BEETHOVEN by Rosemary Hughes
BRAHMS by Kathleen Dale
CHOPIN by Derek Melville
HANDEL by Charles Cudworth
HAYDN by Brian Redfern
MOZART by Alec Hyatt King

CHOPIN

A biography, with a survey of
books, editions and recordings

by
Derek Melville

CLIVE BINGLEY   &   LINNET BOOKS
LONDON   HAMDEN · CONN

FIRST PUBLISHED 1977 BY CLIVE BINGLEY LTD
16 PEMBRIDGE ROAD LONDON W11
SIMULTANEOUSLY PUBLISHED IN THE USA BY LINNET BOOKS
AN IMPRINT OF THE SHOE STRING PRESS INC
995 SHERMAN AVENUE HAMDEN CONNECTICUT 06514
SET IN 12 ON 13 POINT ALDINE ROMAN BY ALLSET
AND PRINTED AND BOUND IN THE UK BY
REDWOOD BURN LTD OF TROWBRIDGE AND ESHER
COPYRIGHT ©DEREK MELVILLE 1977
ALL RIGHTS RESERVED
BINGLEY ISBN: 0-85157-230-8
LINNET ISBN: 0-208-01542-6

Library of Congress Cataloguing in Publication Data

Melville, Derek.
    Chopin: a biography, with a survey of books,
editions and recordings.

    (Concertgoer's companions)
    Includes index.
    1. Chopin, Fryderyk Franciszek, 1810-1849.
2. Chopin, Fryderyk Franciszek, 1810-1849—Bibliography.
3. Composers—Biography.
ML410.C54M47   786.1'092'4 [B]   76-53009
ISBN 0-208-01542-6

Contents

For Jean with love

My thanks are due to Mrs Kathleen Dale, who was always ready with helpful advice and who typed the book for me; to Mr Alan Pummel, Librarian of the Norwich Central Lending Library, for his kind assistance in obtaining for me numerous books on Chopin; and to Mr Mark Rumary for his sustained help and encouragement. Quotations in the text are from *Chopin's letters,* collected by Henryk Opienski, translated by E L Voynich (Alfred A Knopf, 1932) and *Selected correspondence of Fryderyk Chopin,* translated and edited by Arthur Hedley (Heinemann, 1962).

DM   Yoxford, Suffolk, 1976

Chopin's life

THE EXILE AND THE MAN

On November 2 1830 Fryderyk Chopin, aged twenty, left Warsaw on his way to Vienna for his second visit to the Austrian capital; he was never to return to Poland.

During the preceding months he had a presentiment that he would not see his home again. This voluntary exile from the land that he loved had much to do with the intensely strong nationalistic side of his music. For Chopin, absence truly made the heart grow fonder. Exile sharpened his patriotism and increased his nostalgia for Poland. These feelings never left him throughout his all-too-short life, and as a result he became, and still is, Poland's greatest ambassador.

Since Chopin died in 1849, certain aspects of his life and personality have been given undue prominence at the expense of others. His ill-health, for example, which dates from his sojourn in Majorca in 1838, and the fact that his circle of friends and pupils in Paris came mainly from the aristocracy. Some of George Sand's pronouncements on Chopin are not flattering: she was responsible for making him appear almost feeble-minded, as she always stressed and made much of any kind of weakness in him. These facts have inevitably produced a distorted picture of the man, and this distortion affected the judgement of his music by Victorian writers. They have in turn been quoted by successive generations and, consequently, the most extraordinary

7

nonsense has been written about some of his music. The 'musical nonsense' has been used again to portray his character, which has often been described as weak and effeminate.

Nothing could be further from the truth. His ill-health caused him to be trying and sometimes irritable but he did endeavour to hide it from all but those nearest to him. His circle of friends came by no means solely from the aristocracy in Paris. Many were expatriate Poles, musicians and artists, and not all his pupils were society ladies. George Sand, apart from being a novelist, was an expert at putting herself in a good light at the expense of others. Chopin did not escape.

Far more of his true character and personality can be gleaned from his letters than from most biographies, and if this knowledge is added to a study of the music he wrote, the picture becomes even clearer. This is not in any way to ignore the facts of his life and contemporary reports of him which appear in the biographies, but they are not sufficient, and many are second-hand. Inevitably they stray, or could have strayed, into the world of fiction, often, no doubt, by accident.

Obviously, his letters are more adult at thirty than at twenty. Whereas the earlier ones were often full of youthful exuberance, by the time he was thirty-seven they have altered again and are preoccupied with his own and other people's troubles. Ill-health was probably one reason for this, but also, after he had parted from George Sand in 1847, he became very depressed and often bitter about her. Besides, he then felt increasingly his self-imposed exile from his homeland. Yet most of his letters show interest and concern for other people.

We can see that in spite of these misfortunes, his underlying personality did not really alter throughout his life. He was a kind, quiet, gentle, and sensitive man; though somewhat shy, there was also a very gay and spirited side to his nature. He had a quick sense both of humour and of the ridiculous, but there was also a melancholic and indeterminate side which came to the fore in the face of adversity and ill health. He was unquestionably modest, even if he did realise his own worth, but he did not always suffer fools gladly, particularly musical ones. During his last years he was sometimes difficult and impatient, but this,

8

again, was due to his poor health and to the fact that he probably worked beyond his strength.

He was of medium height, but a very slight figure. In 1840 he weighed only about seven stone. He had fair hair, blue grey eyes and an aquiline nose. His appearance in 1833 was distinguished, as can be seen from Engelman's engraving of a lost portrait by Vigneron. As his health declined, his looks altered considerably. There is a photograph taken in 1849 which is not really very like the drawing by Winterhalter, made the previous year and which Chopin himself said was a good likeness. The artist Delacroix and Chopin were great friends, and there is no doubt that the former's painting of him, which is in the Louvre, shows a Chopin that few had the chance of seeing. His bearing was aristocratic and somewhat aloof to all but his closest friends. Except possibly to his own countrymen he was not easily accessible. He has been described by some as being 'strait-laced'.

Chopin was fastidious in his dress and liked to be fashionably but not flamboyantly attired. He had good taste in decoration, and liked eighteenth-century furniture at a time when it was unfashionable. He seems to have been particular in observing proprieties. George Sand said of him, 'He is afraid of society'. Chopin was not the dreamy poetic figure often imagined; he was a hard-working composer who achieved an enormous amount, in spite of illness. He pushed back the boundaries of music and made the greatest single contribution to harmonic development in the first half of the nineteenth century.

THE MUSICAL CHILD IN WARSAW

Fryderyk Chopin was born at Zelazowa Wola, a small village thirty-four miles from Warsaw, on March 1 1810, the second of four children, and only son of Nicholas Chopin (1771-1844) and Tekla Justyna Chopin, nee Krzyżanowska (1782-1861). He was christened Fryderyk Franciszek at Brochow church on April 23 1810. Even though the parish register gives the date of his birth as February 22, Chopin himself, and all his family, always maintained that it was March 1. Although he was always

9

known as Frédéric to his contemporaries, and subsequent biographers use this form, the Polish style is more correct.

He was fortunate in both his parents, not least that his father was French, born at Marainville in the Vosges, and that his mother was Polish, born at, or near, Dlugie in Poland. It was the fusion of French and Polish qualities in him, coupled with musical genius, which produced a unique personality. His mother was of a gentle and quiet disposition, and her greatest joy was to provide a happy and peaceful home for her family, whilst his father Nicholas was a man of the highest integrity, revered by all who knew him. He was the son of a vine-grower and wheelwright, one François Chopin, born in 1738, who in turn was the son of a vine-grower, Nicholas Chopin.

The younger Nicholas left France at the age of sixteen and went to Poland, where he became a clerk in a tobacco factory that was run by a Frenchman. In the midst of political uncertainty this factory went bankrupt, and in 1794 Nicholas joined the Polish National Guard. Later on he became tutor to various Polish families, and finally to the children of Count Skarbek at Zelazowa Wola, where he met Justyna, his future wife (a relation of the Skarbek family), whom he married in 1806. Nicholas cut himself off from his family in Lorraine, and when, much later, Chopin was living in Paris, it is very unlikely he knew that he had two aunts who lived at Marainville. Nicholas, having risen in the world, probably felt that his sisters might be an embarrassment to his son. He never spoke of his family.

Early in 1810, Nicholas moved with his wife, his daughter Ludwika (1807-1855) and his infant son to Warsaw, where he became professor of French at the newly opened Lyceum, and also a teacher of French at the School of Artillery and Military Engineering. In 1811 the third child Isabella was born. The youngest, Emilia, born a year later, lived only until she was fourteen and died of consumption. Both the other sisters married, but only Ludwika had children—three boys and a girl. The family lived in the centre of Warsaw which, by this time in its history, was little more than a provincial town, because Poland had been crushed by the Russians. It was for this reason

10

that Chopin felt that he had to leave it in 1830 if he was to make his mark in the world. As can be seen from their correspondence, they were a devoted family, and although he began to feel very dissatisfied with Warsaw, when the time came it was nevertheless a great wrench to leave his home.

As a very young child Fryderyk was extremely sensitive to music, which affected him deeply. He would often end up in tears when he heard his mother sing or play the piano. He himself began to play at the age of four or five, encouraged by his mother. By the time he was six he improvised to a remarkable degree, which was the beginning of his composing. His handwriting at this time was astonishingly mature, as can be seen from the earliest example, a birthday greeting written to his father in 1816. In this same year his parents felt he should have a teacher who would guide him. They were fortunate to find Adalbert Zywny, and it was he who imparted to the boy his love of J S Bach. Zywny was really a violinist, but he was most probably able to guide Fryderyk much more successfully than a hidebound stereotyped piano teacher, allowing the child's phenomenal technical ability to develop naturally without interference.

Chopin's lessons with Zywny ceased after he was twelve; he began to have lessons in harmony and counterpoint with Joseph Elsner, a Polish composer of German origin and head of the conservatoire in Warsaw. He also learned from Elsner how to write out his compositions for himself; until this time he had had to rely on Zywny to do it for him. Again, Fryderyk was extremely lucky to have had such a wise teacher as Elsner, who had realised at the outset that he was dealing with a musical genius. When others found fault with Fryderyk for breaking the 'rules', Elsner said: 'Leave him alone, he follows an unusual path because his gifts are unusual. He does not follow any traditional method closely, because he has a method of his own, and he will reveal in his works an originality that has never been met before in such a high degree.'

Before this, however, Fryderyk's first published work appeared in 1817, a Polonaise in G minor which was dedicated to

11

the Countess Victoria Skarbek, the daughter of his god-parents. The following year he made his first appearance as a pianist in public, playing a concerto by Gyrowetz at a charity concert. It was after this concert that, when asked what the audience enjoyed most, he is supposed to have said without hesitation 'my collar, Mamma', quite unconscious that his playing was extraordinary even at this early age. The singer Angelica Catalani visited Warsaw in 1820 and asked to hear him play. She was so impressed that she gave him a gold watch with her name and his inscribed on it.

The Grand Duke Constantine, who was virtually Poland's ruler, and his wife Princess Lowicka often invited the boy to come and play, sending the ducal carriage for him. He composed a march for the duke, who had it scored for a military band but without the composer's name. When he was improvising, Fryderyk was inclined to look upwards at the ceiling and the Grand Duke once asked him if he saw the notes up there. In 1825 the Tsar Alexander I came to Warsaw and attended a concert at which Fryderyk played; afterwards he gave him a diamond ring. There is no lack of evidence that his musical ability was appreciated; for instance, his op 1, the Rondo in C minor, was published at this time in Warsaw.

THE VACILLATIONS OF YOUTH

His parents were anxious that his general studies should not be neglected, and until he was sixteen he had the normal education of the day. As a result of working so hard at his music as well, he overtaxed himself when he was about sixteen. His youngest sister Emilia was by now gravely ill with consumption, and in an effort to save her life and restore Fryderyk's health, it was decided that Justyna should take both them and Ludwika to Reinertz in Silesia for the 'whey cure' and the waters. It was while they were there that Fryderyk played at the Kurhaus for the benefit of two children whose father had died and left them destitute. The death of his sister Emilia the following year

12

upset him considerably, as can be seen from a letter to Jan Bialoblocki about a month before she died. Three years later in 1830 he headed a letter to his greatest friend, Tytus Woyciechowski, 'Anniversary of Emilia's death'.

When Fryderyk was sixteen-and-a-half he gave up attending the Lyceum, and he wrote to a friend: 'It would be silly to sit at a desk for six hours a day when the German-Polish doctors have told me to walk as much as possible. It would be stupid to sit through the same lessons again when I can be learning something new this year. I am going to Elsner for strict counterpoint six hours a week. I go to lectures by Brodziński, Bentkowski and others, on subjects connected in any way with music. I go to bed at nine o'clock. All parties and dances are off. I drink emetic waters on Malcz's orders, and eat nothing but oatmeal—like a horse.'

By now he had composed as many as twenty works, including several sets of variations, six polonaises and the same number of mazurkas. The two latter are important in that they show how early Fryderyk began to absorb his national music. He had plenty of opportunities for doing this when he went to stay in the country with his godmother at Stryzewo, and at Sokolowo with his school-friend Jan Bialoblocki. He also went for holidays to his birthplace Zelazowa Wola, and to Szafarnia, whence he sent letters home in the form of a newspaper which he called the 'Szafarnia courier', and himself 'M Pichon'. In one, he mentions that he heard a girl singing a mazurka at the top of her voice, and that he paid her three sous to sing it again because he could not hear the words. (Mazurkas are sung as well as danced in Poland.)

The Rondo à la Mazur, op 5, which was written when Fryderyk was sixteen, is perhaps the first work that could be described as typical of his style. The following year the Mazurka op 68 no 2 and the Nocturne op 72 no 1 appeared. This latter work is extraordinarily mature, melodically and harmonically, and is probably connected with the death of his sister Emilia. This year, 1827, saw the beginning of serious composition. He wrote the Variations on Mozart's 'Là ci darem' from

13

Don Giovanni for piano and orchestra, which were published three years later by Haslinger in Vienna. Without doubt this set of variations was his first major composition and unmistakably original in style. It was dedicated to Tytus Woyciechowski, with whom Chopin seems to have been tremendously infatuated. But his feelings at this time appear to be ambivalent; it is hardly possible to assess how deep they were and how long they lasted. Despite his affection for Maria Wodzińska, Delphina Potocka, and his love for George Sand, his attachment to some of his own sex stands out most clearly in many of his letters. It may account for his seeming lack of drive towards the opposite sex, and explain why he vacillated and never married. Although no really passionate letters to any women are extant, some may possibly come to light. It has been suggested that the style of writing and address in use between men at that time is misleading. Even if this is so, it does not account for Fryderyk's heartfelt outpouring in his letters to Tytus. There are seventeen letlets to him, written between December 1828 and December 1831, in which no woman could have expressed herself more passionately.

In an extraordinary letter from George Sand to Albert Grzymala, which was written in June 1838 (and is mentioned again later) she writes: 'I want to tell you that one thing only in him [Chopin] displeased me; namely, he had false reasons for abstaining. Until then, I found it beautiful that he should abstain out of respect for me, out of timidity, or even out of faithfulness for someone else . . . But at your house, just as he was leaving, and as if he wished to resist a last temptation, he said a few words that did not fit in with my ideas. He seemed, like the pious, to despise *human* coarseness, and to blush at the temptations he had had, and to fear to sully our love by any further transport. This view of the last embrace of love has always repelled me. If the last embrace is not as holy, as pure, as consecrated as the rest, there is no virtue in abstention . . . He said, I think, that *certain acts* could mar a memory. Tell me that was stupid, and he did not mean it . . . Who then is the unfortunate woman who has left him with such an

14

impression of physical love?' Chopin's outward manner and his courtesy towards women were impeccable, but he seems, mostly, to have been indifferent to them. This partially explains why women flocked round him and why he was such a success with them; though of course, his music and his playing were the main reasons for his appeal.

Early in 1829 Chopin imagined himself in love with a young singer, Constantia Gladkowska, who was a student at the conservatoire in Warsaw and the same age as himself. It was six months before he even mentioned her to Tytus. He first writes to him of his 'ideal' and admits he has worshipped her for six months without ever speaking or writing to her. Such is far from being the case where his feelings for Tytus were concerned. There is no certainty at any time that his true emotions were really involved with Constantia. It appears to have been much more the idea of being in love with her that mattered to him, and even how it should appear to other people. It could have been a conscious or an unconscious 'blind'. Chopin seems to have realised, in the end, that Tytus did not reciprocate his ardent feelings although he was obviously fond of him. Before this, however, in the summer of 1828 after visiting various friends at Sanniki, Strzyzewo and Danzig, he returned home to Warsaw to find that a friend of his father's, Dr Jarocki, a zoology professor, had suggested that Chopin should be allowed to go with him to Berlin where he was to attend a scientific congress. Chopin was tremendously excited at the thought of hearing some good music and opera, and of possibly meeting Mendelssohn. They set off on September 9 1828 and after five days in a coach they arrived in Berlin, 'this much too big town', and put up at the Kronprinz Hotel. He saw Spontini and Mendelssohn, but was too shy to introduce himself. He heard amongst other things Cimarosa's *Il matrimonio segreto*, Weber's *Freischütz*, which he was very keen to hear and see, and Handel's *Ode for St Cecilia's Day*. This last work, he wrote, 'came nearest to the idea that I have formed of great music'.

After fourteen days in Berlin, Chopin and Jarocki returned home via Poznan, where they stayed with Prince Radziwill and dined with Archbishop Wolicki. The prince, who played the 'cello, showed great interest in the newly finished first movement of the Trio op 8; the work was ultimately dedicated to him. On the journey home, while waiting for a change of horses, Chopin found a piano at the inn and began to play to pass the time. Gradually all his fellow travellers came in to listen to him, including a German who had annoyed them all by smoking his pipe in the night. The story goes that this man was now so amazed and enraptured by what he heard that he allowed his pipe to go out. When the horses were ready, the whole company begged Chopin to continue playing; finally he was given wine and sweetmeats and carried in triumph by the innkeeper to the coach. It is said that Chopin never forgot this incident because giving pleasure to those few people meant more to him than playing to a large audience.

It was not until his return from Berlin that Chopin was given a room of his own to work in with an old piano in it. This must have made all the difference to him, and it is reflected in the amount and scope of the music he wrote in the following year; four of the Studies from op 10 (nos 8, 9, 10 and 11) and the Concerto in F minor op 21. Yet even before he had this work-room of his own he managed to create works like the Rondo for two pianos op 73, the first movement of the Trio op 8, and the Variations op 2, which has an orchestral accompaniment.

In 1829 Chopin met Hummel when he came to Warsaw. He was a distinguished pianist and composer whose music shows a strong Mozartian influence, not surprisingly, since he lived and studied with him for two of his formative years. Chopin always professed great admiration for Hummel's music. Nevertheless his influence on Chopin, like that of Field's, has perhaps been overstressed. Chopin adopted some pianistic patterns and devices which can be found not only in the concertos of both the older men, but also in works by Spohr and Kalkbrenner. Common to all four composers was a certain manner of superficial pianistic display, which Chopin transformed into an organic part of the music and made peculiarly his own. It is most

16

noticeable in his concertos and the other few works with orchestra. But it is important to realise that Chopin's basic musical forbears were J S Bach, Mozart and Schubert, and that fundamentally he was classical in outlook, not romantic; he hated the romantic movement. Paganini also came to Warsaw during this year, and though there is no record of Chopin's meeting him, his miraculous playing may be said to have inspired the composition of some of the Studies of op 10.

FIRST VISIT TO VIENNA

The visit to Berlin had made Chopin restless and had given him a taste for the outside world, so that when he learnt that three of his friends—Hube, Celiński and Maciejowski—were going to Vienna, he implored his father to let him go with them. The necessary money was found and Chopin was wildly excited at the prospect. He set off for Vienna with his friends in July 1829, arrived on July 31 and stayed away from Warsaw for about two months. Vienna had been the musical centre of the world since the time of Haydn and Mozart, but it began to decline after Beethoven's death in 1827 and Schubert's a year later. Nevertheless when Chopin first arrived, it was still of great importance, particularly to a young musician on the threshold of his career.

Amongst other things, Chopin wanted to meet the Viennese publisher Haslinger, who had been considering several of his works for some time, including the op 2 Variations and the Sonata op 4 (sent to him by Elsner). No doubt the idea of playing in public or to influential patrons was also in his mind. That he took eight days to be persuaded to give a concert and only three days to prepare for it hardly seems possible. It was not a particularly good time, for the season was over and many people were away. However, he was pressed by the musical élite of Vienna, including Haslinger, to go ahead and give not one concert, but two.

17

He made his début at the Imperial Court Theatre on August 11. He played the op 2 Variations, and the Krakowiak op 15 was to have been the other work, but the manuscript of the orchestral parts was neither correct nor legible. The orchestra made such difficulties at the rehearsal that Chopin abandoned playing it and decided to improvise on a theme from Boïeldieu's opera *La dame blanche*, which he had heard a few nights before. He did a second improvisation, using the Polish song *Chmiel*, which electrified the audience. Before the second concert his compatriot Nidecki looked through and corrected the orchestral parts of the Krakowiak, which he played a week later. He wrote: 'If I was well received the first time, it was still better yesterday'. The only criticism was that he played too softly or 'too delicately for people used to the piano-pounding of the artists here'. He goes on: 'I expect to find this reproach in the paper, especially as the editor's daughter thumps frightfully. It doesn't matter, there has always got to be a *but* somewhere, and I should rather it were that one than have people say I played too loudly.'

After the concerts Haslinger told Chopin that the Variations op 2 would be published in five weeks' time, but they did not in fact appear until January 1830. Blahetka, a journalist, said to Chopin before he left that he was surprised at his learning all that he had in Warsaw. Chopin replied, 'under Zywny and Elsner even the greatest donkey could learn'.

While he was in Vienna he met Czerny, whom he describes as 'more sensitive than any of his compositions'. He got on well with him and they played duets together. Chopin left before the notices of the two concerts appeared, but the Viennese press was enthusiastic. He was described as 'a master of the first rank, with his exquisite delicacy of touch, indescribable finger dexterity, and the deep feeling shown by his command of shading. His interpretations and his compositions both bear the stamp of genius . . . [he] appears on the horizon like a most brilliant meteor.' Another notice said 'his touch . . . had little brilliance comparable with the virtuosos who wish to conquer with their first few bars'. One alleged 'defect' was

that Chopin failed to accent the beginning of each musical
phrase, a fairly certain indication of the exceedingly unmu-
sical, not to say vulgar style of playing accepted at that time.

FAREWELL TO POLAND

Chopin left Vienna at nine in the evening of August 19. He
travelled via Prague and Dresden and arrived back in Warsaw
in September. He now became even more restless at home,
but had to wait thirteen months before he left Warsaw again,
and then for the last time. Meanwhile, he was writing his first
Piano Concerto, the F minor, which, as it was published six
years later in 1836 and after the one in E minor, is known as
no 2. (The reason for the delay in publication was that the orchestral parts were lost, and he found it a very uncongenial task
to write them out again.) Chopin is said to have had a preference for the F minor concerto; certainly the middle section of
the slow movement contains a most remarkable piece of orchestration. Tovey describes it 'as fine a piece of instrumentation
as Berlioz could have chosen to quote in his famous treatise'.
Yet for all that, it is astonishingly simple and direct; a dramatic
recitative for piano with the two hands in unison, and an orchestral accompaniment of tremolo strings with double-bass
pizzicati. This accompaniment heightens its already dramatic
quality, particularly as it interrupts an exquisite aria for the
piano.
   In October Chopin's father sent him off to Antonin, Prince
Radziwill's estate near Poznan, where he spent only a week,
but wrote a polonaise for 'cello and piano for the Prince and
his daughter Princess Wanda. Nicholas Chopin was anxious
that his son should go to Berlin to continue his studies and
broaden his outlook, and the Radziwills had offered hospitality in their palace. Chopin, however, had other ideas, and
was keen to return to Vienna, where he had met with such success. It was not until March 17 1830 that he gave his first public concert in Warsaw, at which he played the F minor concerto

and the Fantasia on Polish airs op 13, which he had written in November 1828. The latter is an exhilarating work of great charm, and deserves to be heard more often.

It is interesting to learn that Chopin had several rehearsals of the concerto, including a performance at his home with a string quartet, before the public one took place. The concert had to be repeated five days later; at both of them, all the seats were sold out in advance. It was a resounding success. At the first concert he had used his own piano, probably a Bucholtz, which had a rounded tone, as a good piano in proper condition should have; at the second, he was persuaded to use a Graf from Vienna, which was more strident and which he did not like so much, although the audience preferred it. As was the custom in those days, the first movement was separated from the adagio and rondo by another item, a divertissement for French horn by Görner.

Chopin spent much of the next four or five months writing the E minor Piano Concerto, and he had great difficulty in finishing it: 'I shall finish the opening allegro of the second concerto before the holidays', he wrote on March 27 1830. The concerto is dedicated to Kalkbrenner (whom Chopin was to meet two years later in Paris), then one of the first pianists in Europe. Chopin may well have used as a model for his own E minor concerto some of the first movement of Kalkbrenner's Piano Concerto no 1 in D minor op 61. The orchestration and the subordinate role that the orchestra plays in accompanying the piano, with background harmony, is markedly like that in Kalkbrenner's concerto.

Chopin went to stay at Poturzyn, Tytus' estate, and poured out his troubles and uncertainties to his friend. He became very indeterminate about making plans to leave Warsaw and set off again for Vienna, possibly because of his feelings for Tytus. By now he had become well acquainted with Constantia Gladkowska and though they exchanged rings, there was never any promise between them. When Karasowski's *Life of Chopin* was read to her as an old lady (she had become blind in 1845), she expressed complete surprise that she had appeared to mean so much to Chopin. This is because he was not really in love with her, as he admits in a letter to Tytus; he never wrote to her as he did to Tytus himself.

It becomes increasingly clear that at this time Tytus was the object of his affection and that Chopin realised how hopeless this was. Yet he was unable to resist making plans. He would meet Tytus on foreign soil after he finally leaves for Vienna, for Tytus was obviously fond of him and had agreed to go with him. He would not travel from Poland with him, as 'it would spoil the moment when we embrace each other abroad for the first time'. No differences in language, or the style of 150 years ago can possibly alter the meaning or sense of the following letter: 'I will send it [his portrait] to you, as soon as possible; if you want it, you shall have it; but no one else except you shall have my portrait. There is only one other person to whom I would give it; and even then to you first, for you are my dearest. No one but myself has read your letter. As always, I carry your letters about with me . . . What joy it will be . . . to get out your letter and really convince myself that you care for me, or at least to look at the handwriting and signature of the person I love so much'.

Again, on May 12 1830 Chopin wrote: 'No, you don't know how much I love you, I can't show it to you in any way, and I have wished for so long that you could know. Ah, what would I not give, just to press your hand, you can't guess—half of my wretched life.' And a little later: 'I am going to wash now; don't kiss me, I'm not washed yet. You? If I were smeared with the oils of Byzantium, you would not kiss me unless I forced you to it by magnetism. There's some kind of power in nature. Today you will dream of kissing me! I have got to pay you out for the horrible dream you gave me last night.'

On September 18 1830, less than a month before he left, he wrote: 'it's no use, I know that I love you and want you to love me always more and more.' He didn't really 'get over' Tytus until after he was living in Paris.

The op 2 Variations were published and arrived from Vienna in July. After playing them at a small concert given by a singer, Mme Meyer, Chopin left Warsaw to go and stay again at

Poturzyn with Tytus. He returned for Constantia's début in Paër's *Agnese* and for a last visit to Zelazowa Wola, but most of the time he was preoccupied with finishing the E minor concerto. Finally, he had a private rehearsal of the concerto at home towards the end of September, and gave his farewell concert in Warsaw on October 11 1830, at which he played the E minor concerto, or, as he put it, 'which I just reeled off; one can do that on a Streicher piano'. Chopin would have found a Streicher, with its lighter touch, perhaps even easier to play than a Graf. But both these Viennese pianos would have seemed very light after any Polish or German make, which would have almost certainly had the much heavier English action. Also he liked the fuller tone which a piano with an English action had, compared with the shallow tone of the Viennese makers. Without doubt this is one reason why Chopin preferred Pleyel's pianos, because they had a beautiful singing tone and an English action to which he had been accustomed. He said in this same letter that the conductor Soliva 'succeeded so well in keeping us together that I can assure you I have never before managed to play so well with orchestra'. Two singers, Mlle Wolkow, 'dressed in sky blue and looking like an angel', and Constantia Gladkowska, 'dressed in white with roses in her hair', enhanced the concert by each singing an aria, and Chopin ended with his Fantasia on Polish airs op 13. The rest of October was spent in preparations for his departure on November 2. Nicholas Chopin had tried to get a state grant to help with the expense of sending his son abroad, but the application was refused. The stage coach to Vienna stopped at Wola, just outside Warsaw, where Elsner with a choir sang a cantata he had composed especially for the occasion to wish Chopin luck. It must have been very moving for him, as the hardest thing of all was to say goodbye to his family.

FRUSTRATION IN VIENNA

Chopin met Tytus at Kalisz, then on the border of Poland, whence they journeyed to Breslau, where Chopin played the adagio and rondo of the E minor concerto at an impromptu concert. After four days they left for Dresden; there, they attended the opera and were besieged with invitations, and finally arrived in Vienna on November 23 1830. Within a week came the news of the revolt against the Russians which had broken out in Warsaw on November 29. Tytus set out for home at once, leaving Chopin behind; it is not certain whether the latter then tried to follow Tytus but turned back again.

Chopin found lodgings in the centre of Vienna with which he was very pleased, because although he was on the fourth floor, they were close to the opera-house and to various music shops.

Unfortunately, he was quickly disillusioned by lack of real interest and support; there was much talk about giving a public concert, but that was all. He was determined not to play without a fee, which he had done on his first visit. Haslinger would not publish any more of his music; he may have lost money on the op 2 Variations because they were, as Sir Charles Hallé remarked, 'so dreadfully difficult that I have to study it bar by bar . . . these variations are far from being considered among his most difficult works, from which God preserve us! ' Chopin began to rue the day he left Warsaw, and to hate the endless evening parties and dances he felt obliged to attend. He was lonely and homesick already, and his only relief was to compose and play on 'Graf's dull piano'.

The first works that he wrote in Vienna were the four Mazurkas of op 6, which were immediately followed by the five of op 7, the first fruits of his exile. The Mazurkas were followed by the first Waltz to be published, op 18, inspired no doubt by his surroundings, for it is the most Viennese of all the waltzes. Next he wrote three Polish songs, which were in turn followed by the sad, not to say gloomy Waltz in A minor op 34 no 2, and finally, the impassioned Scherzo in B minor op 20. This—like the letters of these months—seems to rail at his unsatisfactory circumstances in Vienna, and had for its subject, in the slow middle section, the Polish carol 'Lullaby little Jesus'.

Chopin played twice more in Vienna. At a concert given by the singer Garzia-Vestris he performed the E minor concerto as a piano solo on April 4 1831, and played it again on June 11 with an orchestra. Neither concert did him the slightest good or brought him very much money which, by this time, he badly needed, as he was worried at being a drain on his father's resources. He had become very melancholy and apathetic, not to say neurotic, and at last decided to leave Vienna. His stay of about eight months had proved fruitless; but one good thing to come out of it was that it sent him on his way to Paris. He had to give up the idea of going to Italy because there, too, unrest and revolt were rife. As Chopin was not allowed by the Russian embassy to go to France, to which so many Polish exiles had fled, his passport was marked 'Munich'. 'Never mind', he wrote to his parents, 'only let M. Maison, the French ambassador, sign it.'

Cholera was rife in Vienna, and this held up Chopin's departure, as he had to obtain a health certificate before he could be allowed to cross the Bavarian frontier. Having travelled to Munich via Salzburg, he had to wait for money from his father to arrive; so he arranged a concert on August 28 and played the E minor concerto and Fantasia on Polish airs. His passport was finally marked: 'en passant par Paris à Londres'. He used to make a joke about it in the years to come when he lived in Paris, saying, 'I am only passing through!'

Just a week later in Stuttgart the news came that Warsaw had fallen. This was the most bitter blow of all and nearly unhinged his mind, for he was already prostrate with grief and worry over his family. His hatred of the Russians, overwhelming despair, but above all, terrific defiance, are all surely pictured both in the Etude in C minor op 10 no 12, and in the coda of the G minor Ballade, also written at this time. Soon he left Stuttgart, and arrived in Paris in the third week of September 1831.

PARIS: MUSICAL CENTRE OF THE WORLD

For the next nineteen years—that is, for the rest of his life— Paris was to be Chopin's home and in it he had nine different addresses. In his first letter from there written on November 18 1831 to Alfons Kumelski, a Polish friend in Berlin whom he had met in Vienna, he says: 'I reached Paris quite safely although it cost me a lot, and I am delighted with what I have found. I have the finest musicians and opera in the world. I know Rossini, Cherubini, Paër, etc; and shall perhaps stay here longer than I intended—not because things have been too easy for me but because they may gradually turn out well. You, however, are the lucky one—you are drawing near home while I, perhaps, may never see my people again.' This, after one year away! He goes on to say that there is more mud in Paris than it is possible to imagine, that his rooms are on the fifth floor and he can see from Montmartre to the Panthéon, and that people envy him his view but not his stairs.

Chopin had come to know the pianist Kalkbrenner who was anxious to make him his pupil for three years. At first he had such great admiration for Kalkbrenner's playing that he seriously considered the proposition. His father, his sister Louise, and Elsner all wrote to him at once to dissuade him from such a plan. It was, of course, ridiculous, and after one or two lessons Kalkbrenner admitted that three years was too long. When he realised that Chopin was undecided, he was willing to relax his three-year course, for he was astute enough to realise that it would be enormously to his advantage if he could say that Chopin was his pupil. But it only needed Liszt and Hiller to impress up-on Chopin that he was already a finer pianist than Kalkbrenner, for him to discontinue having any lessons at all. Nevertheless, to a certain extent, Chopin kept in with Kalkbrenner, who was a partner in the firm of Pleyel, one of the foremost of French pianoforte makers. Kalkbrenner and Pleyel helped to arrange Chopin's first concert in Paris.

Let us return to Chopin's reactions to the musical scene in Paris and to some of the musicians he met. A letter to Tytus, written December 12 1831, mentions that Dr Malfatti of Vienna, who was physician to both Beethoven and the Emperor and had befriended Chopin there, gave him an introduction to Paër, through whom, as already mentioned, he got to know Rossini, Cherubini and Kalkbrenner. He met the pianists Liszt, Herz and Hiller, all of whom he described as being zero beside Kalk-brenner. In this same letter Chopin confesses that he had him-self sometimes played like Herz (a brilliant but rather shallow pianist), but said that he wished to play like Kalkbrenner: 'It is hard to describe his calm, enchanting touch, his incomparable evenness'.

Chopin was most impressed by the Paris opera and the singers Lablache, Pasta and Malibran; he also mentioned Pleyel's pianos, which were *non plus ultra*. In his next letter to Tytus, of Dec-ember 25 1831, he said that his concert had to be put off until January 15. In point of fact he did not give it till February 26 1832, because there had been great difficulties in engaging the singers, and Kalkbrenner himself was ill. Chopin tells how he has to suffer a compatriot who comes to see him and 'bangs and pounds without meaning, throws himself about, crosses his hands [and] clatters on one key for five minutes'. He went on, 'If ever I have seen a clear picture of charlatanism or stupidity in art, it is now . . . most of all he enrages me with his collec-tion of pothouse tunes put together without the slightest know-ledge of harmony or prosody, but which he calls a collection of Polish songs. You know how I have longed to feel our national music, and to some extent have succeeded.' He dis-posed of Liszt by saying 'the themes of his compositions will repose with the newspapers'. Describing Berlioz, Chopin is supposed to have dipped his pen in the ink, bent the nib back-wards so that it spattered the MS paper, and said, 'that is how Berlioz composes'. For the second time (the first was in Vienna) he complained that his health was bad, which was probably nothing more than a generally neurotic state, but he added that perhaps he would never see Tytus again. In this he was right.

CONCERTS AND LESSONS IN PARIS

At Chopin's first concert in Paris both Mendelssohn and Liszt were present, the latter in the front row. Liszt said that the enthusiastic applause was renewed again and again, but that it scarcely sufficed to express his own enchantment. Chopin received a good notice from Fétis in the *Revue musicale* of March 3 1832, but financially the concert was a failure. He played at a charity concert on May 20, where the audience was a fashionable one, whereas at his own first recital the audience had consisted of Poles and musicians.

Fairly soon after this he met, by chance, Prince Valentine Radziwill, who invited him to come to a soirée given by Baron de Rothschild, and the Baroness asked Chopin if he would play. He was an instant success and was inundated with requests for lessons from many society ladies. From this moment his financial position was secure, and unlike other contemporary musicians, including even Liszt, he was accepted in society. In a letter to Dominic Dziewanowski, a Polish friend who was living in Berlin, Chopin wrote: 'I have got into the highest society; I sit with ambassadors, princes, ministers; and even don't know how it came about, because I did not try for it. It is a most necessary thing for me, because good taste is supposed to depend on it. At once you have a bigger talent if you have been heard at the English or the Austrian embassy; . . . I have five lessons to give today; you think I am making a fortune? Carriages and white gloves cost more, and without them one would not be in good taste.'

Chopin, like Liszt, charged twenty francs a lesson, which was expensive, whereas Kalkbrenner asked only ten to twelve francs. Chopin's success began in the spring of 1832 and he was heard frequently in public at this time; not in large concert halls, but at private concerts and in fashionable salons. He began to publish many of the works he had composed in Warsaw and Vienna. Once he became financially secure he was able to compose, and this also considerably supplemented his income. It is fortunate that he did not care for playing in public, as he would then never have had the time or energy to compose as well as teach. Whenever Chopin did play in public, he nearly always played his own works. Naturally, it gave him much more satisfaction to become well known as a composer rather

27

than just as a pianist. Emily Hill, who translated Karasowski's biography of Chopin in 1877, wrote: 'Chopin was supreme in delicacy and finish, it was his distinctive achievement to have attained greatness in the smallest forms'. Yet for a long time the fact that Chopin limited himself to writing only for the piano was considered a defect. It hindered his recognition as one of the world's greatest composers. Now it is seen as being a large part of his greatness.

The publication of the Studies op 10 established Chopin as an outstanding composer for all time at a single stroke. No one before had linked such exquisite music with the technical problems of playing the piano. Even today, performers seldom do them full justice musically. This first set, dedicated to Liszt, was completed in Paris in 1832, three of them, nos 7, 3 and 4, having been written there. A subtle difference can be noticed between these studies, composed after he had met Liszt and Kalkbrenner, and the earlier ones written in Warsaw. There was some very violent, spiteful, almost ludicrous criticism of his music by the German critic Rellstab, who was editor of *Iris im Gebiete der Tonkunst*. Rellstab raved about the ear-splitting discords and ugly distortion of melody in the mazurkas. The nocturnes were likened to Field's held up to a distorting concave mirror; whilst no one should play the studies without having a surgeon at hand. Eleven years later, Rellstab had to ask Liszt for an introduction to the now well-known Chopin before he visited Paris.

The two great piano makers in Paris were Pleyel and Erard. The latter is perhaps the better known of the two, as he invented the double escapement action which is today a standard feature in all modern pianos. Chopin preferred the Pleyel piano because it possessed a unique singing quality which he could control absolutely with the single escapement action. According to Liszt, Chopin summed it up as follows: 'When I am indisposed, I play on one of Erard's pianos and there I easily find a ready-made tone. But when I feel in the right mood and strong enough to find my own tone for myself, I must have one of Pleyel's pianos.' Chopin was more concerned than anyone else before his time, or since, to make the piano sing and to imitate the human voice as much as possible. To use flexible and relaxed hands, and to feel the music as though it were being sung—these, for him, were the prerequisites of good playing. He himself had an immense technical accomplishment, which included an extraordinary control of gradations of tone, and extreme delicacy of touch. It was the combination of these and the impact of his own music (which was completely new and unlike any other), that made him a legend in his own lifetime.

VISITS TO GERMANY—PARIS AGAIN

In 1833 Chopin removed twice, first to 4 Cité Bergère, and then to Rue de la chaussée d'Antin, where he stayed for three years. The following year he felt himself sufficiently established in Paris to be able to leave his pupils and have a holiday. The pianist Ferdinand Hiller had asked Chopin to go with him to the music festival at Aix-la-Chapelle (Aachen) during May. There they met Mendelssohn, who was overjoyed to see them both. He insisted that they should accompany him to Düsseldorf, where, one evening, they repaired to the house of the director of the art school, Schadow. They had spent the day being marched round the town sight-seeing, which Chopin appeared to find rather boring, and then Schadow asked them all in turn to play. Hiller tells us that when it came to Chopin's turn, 'rather doubtful looks were cast at him, but Mendelssohn and I knew he would have his revenge . . . , he had hardly played a few bars before everybody in the room, especially Schadow, was transfixed; nothing like it had ever been heard! '

Chopin returned to Paris to resume his teaching and take up his social life again. He had first met the lovely Countess Delphina Potocka (1807-1887) in Paris in November 1831. She was unhappily married and now lived apart from her husband. Without doubt Chopin became very fond of her, as he himself says in a letter to his family written much later, in April 1847.

She was extremely beautiful and also had a lovely voice; Chopin often used to accompany her. But it is still a matter for conjecture as to whether there was a love affair. Chopin himself strenuously denied it to Liszt. As long ago as 1903, letters from Chopin to Delphina were said to have been preserved, but they were kept under lock and key by the Komar family. Ultimately, they were supposed to have been transferred to the cellars of Raczyński Palace in Warsaw (where Chopin had lived), and were burned with the whole palace in September 1939.

After returning to Paris, Chopin played the second movement of the F minor concerto, which is dedicated to Delphina Potocka, at a concert on December 7 in the conservatoire, at which Berlioz conducted. On December 25 he played at a *Matinée musicale* at the Salle Pleyel with Liszt; they performed a duo by Moscheles, of which the manuscript is lost (it was never published). Chopin was disappointed at his reception, but the lack of enthusiasm at the first of these concerts was due to his music being overshadowed by bigger orchestral works. He was intimidated by a large audience and his whole style of playing was not suited to vast halls. It was, in fact, diametrically opposed to that of a showman like Liszt. Yet he could, when roused, electrify an audience, as he did later at Rouen. In April 1835 he played the E minor concerto and again a duet with Liszt. The concerto was received very indifferently by a restless audience, and the *Gazette musicale* was unable to conceal the fact that Chopin's performance had been a disappointment. Three weeks later, on April 26, he played the Andante Spianato and Polonaise op 22 with considerably more success. Nevertheless he decided that he was not fitted for appearing at large-scale concerts, and thereafter, with one or two exceptions, the audiences seldom exceeded three hundred.

The fact that Chopin was not always successful, that he did not enjoy playing in public, made little or no difference to his reputation as a pianist. This had been established by his playing in Warsaw and Vienna, and in the salons of Paris when he first arrived there. His reputation was also fostered by his

30

musical and literary friends, and really by the whole of Parisian society. Curiously enough, the less he played in public, the more legendary he became. The publication of his music contributed as much to his fame as did his playing. The fact that he played mostly only his own music, helped build up and maintain his great reputation.

In July 1835 he went to Carlsbad to see his parents, who had been sent there to take the waters. They were all overjoyed at being together again. Chopin had left Paris earlier than was necessary so that he could surprise them by being there first. Although he was in the town when they arrived, he was unable to find them; in the end, his parents were awakened at 4 am by a Polish friend who was helping him to look for them. They spent three weeks in Carlsbad, after which they all went as far as Tetschen to stay with friends, and there Chopin composed the Waltz in A flat op 34 no 1. His parents left to return to Warsaw on September 14, and this was the last time Chopin ever saw them. A few days later he left for Dresden, where he met the Wodziński family again, and became attracted to Maria. He wrote for her the Waltz in A flat op 69 no 1. Her three brothers Anton, Casimir and Felix had all been boarders with the Chopin family when they were at school together, and so the Wodzińskis, as a family, were extremely fond of Chopin. This can be gathered from a letter Maria sent to him after he left Dresden.

From there, Chopin went to Leipzig, where he met Schumann and Clara Wieck. He was particularly anxious to hear Clara play, and described her as 'the only woman in Germany who can play my music'. Unfortunately, nothing is known of Chopin's reaction to meeting Schumann, who was, however, enthusiastic about Chopin. Before returning to Paris, he went to stay with his nineteen-year-old pupil Adolf Gutmann, in Heidelberg. There he became ill, a fact which he concealed from his parents, but left them without news for so long that wild rumours began to circulate that he had died. It may have been this illness that prejudiced the Wodzińskis against his engagement to Maria the following year.

31

Back in Paris, he continued his teaching, and composed amongst other works the Nocturne in D flat op 27 no 2, four of the Studies from op 25 (nos 2, 7, 3 and 12) and two of the Preludes (nos 7 and 17). In the summer of 1836 he visited Marienbad, where the Wodzińskis had rented a villa. To begin with, the Countess was genuinely fond of Chopin and would have welcomed him as a son-in-law. Her letters to him are motherly and affectionate, full of advice about going to bed early and wearing warm clothes. She knew that Chopin was not robust and that there would be insuperable opposition to any question of marriage if his health was poor. After he had stayed with them for about six weeks, they all returned to Dresden from Marienbad in the third week of August. Not until September 7, two days before he left for Leipzig, did he propose to Maria. The Countess gave her consent but said it must be kept secret, and she also stressed that it was most important that he should look after his health. Unfortunately, the following winter he had influenza again. Countess Wodzińska had already accused him rather unpleasantly of not taking her advice, to which Chopin replied that he had done so. Gradually letters from her ceased. It is difficult to tell how soon Maria's feelings cooled, for she seems to have been rather shallow, and something of a coquette; being too indolent to write to him very often, she simply added postscripts to her mother's letters. It seems fairly clear that the opposition came from Count Wodziński and his elder brother Palatine Wodziński.

Some biographers have attached great importance to this episode in Chopin's life, because Maria's few letters and those of her mother to him, were found after his death, tied up with ribbon and with 'Moja Biéda' ('my sorrow') written on the envelope. In fact, his sorrow was not very long-lasting. He became run down and listless as a result of his disappointment, but in July Camille Pleyel and Stanislas Kozmian persuaded him to accompany them to London for a complete change. They were there only for a fortnight and met very few people. Chopin played one evening at Broadwood's house, where he was much admired, and by the end of the month he was back in Paris.

In 1837, the second book of Studies op 25 appeared, dedicated to Liszt's mistress the Countess d'Agoult. This set was entirely composed in Paris. It is sometimes incorrectly stated that all the Studies were written at much the same time and that those of op 25 are the less good ones which were rejected from op 10. Nothing could be further from the truth. Compared with op 10, some are more advanced musically and perhaps more interesting. On the whole, they are more delicate and possibly more difficult. After meeting so many other great pianists in the four intervening years, Chopin was probably spurred to even greater technical and musical heights. The following year he played at court, and in March he went to Rouen to play the E minor piano concerto, this time with outstanding success. The atmosphere in the hall was described as 'electric'. The critic Legouvé was present, and wrote: 'When people ask who is the first pianist in Europe, let everyone, like those who have heard you, answer . . . It is Chopin! '

A FATEFUL MEETING

It was in the autumn of 1836 that Chopin first met the novelist who wrote under the name of George Sand (1804-1876). Born d'Amantine-Aurore-Lucile Dupin, her father was Maurice Dupin de Francueil, grandson of the Maréchal de Saxe, son of August II of Poland. Her mother was Sophie-Victoire Delaborde, the daughter of a Paris bird-fancier, and of very humble origin. At the age of eighteen, in order to escape from living with her mother who ill-treated her, George Sand married Baron Casimir Dudevant, but left him nine years later in 1831. On her grandmother's death in 1821 she inherited the estate at Nohant in Berry, where she had been brought up like a boy. Despite her masculinity she had numerous lovers, including Jules Sandeau, Alfred de Musset, Prosper Mérimée and Michel de Bourges.

Chopin was at first repelled by her and asked the pianist Hiller whether she really was a woman, as he was very much inclined to doubt it. George Sand had told Liszt, whom she had met through Marie d'Agoult and who wrote under the name of Daniel Stern, that she would like to meet Chopin. Liszt accordingly arranged an evening at Marie d'Agoult's salon. In his book, however, Liszt states that the first time Chopin and George Sand met was when Liszt himself and a party of his friends, including George Sand, paid a surprise visit to Chopin's apartments. This visit may well have taken place, but probably not until after they had already met.

George Sand invited Chopin to Nohant during 1837 but he did not accept. As she spent the greater part of 1837 at Nohant, it was not really until 1838 that their friendship began. By May of this year she was certainly attracted to Chopin, as can be deduced from letters to Mme Marliani and to Albert Grzymala. The latter was a friend of Chopin's, to whom she wrote a letter of five thousand words (mentioned on page 14), in which she imagined she was expressing her true feelings. She speaks of celestial embraces and voyaging through the empyrean: 'The fleeting moments which we spend there will be so beautiful that they will be worth a whole life spent here below'. The curious thing is that when she wrote to Grzymala saying she did not wish to come between Chopin and Maria Wodzińska or take him away from her, she appears not to have known that the engagement had already been broken off. This seems to suggest that, to begin with, it was a somewhat one-sided affair.

Descriptions of George Sand's appearance vary considerably. In 1838 Balzac described her as having a double chin, not a single white strand in her jet black hair, a dark complexion, and beautiful eyes: 'She goes to bed at six o'clock in the morning and gets up at midday. She is boyish, generous, devoted, *chaste*. She is an excellent mother, adored by her children, but brings up Solange like a little boy and that is not right. She smokes excessively. In short, she is a man, and all the more a man because she wants to be one. Woman attracts, and she repels.' Nevertheless she succeeded, ultimately, in attracting Chopin,

34

and, very probably, in seducing him. George Sand intimated that they were lovers for only a short time because of his physical condition. Their love was replaced by utter devotion on his side, and, to begin with, a great maternal affection on hers.

George Sand's son Maurice, who was fifteen, had been suffering from what was probably rheumatic fever, and the doctors had prescribed wintering in a warmer climate. First, Italy had been suggested, and then, on very bad advice, she decided to go to Majorca. In George Sand's *L'histoire de ma vie* she wrote: 'Chopin whom I saw every day . . . said to me over and over again, that if he were in Maurice's place he would soon be cured himself', and stated that Chopin asked to be taken with them to Majorca. Whether this is really so, is quite another matter. Perhaps the true reason was that she was determined that he should go with them, as otherwise they would have been separated for the whole winter. Yet she considered herself as good as married to Mallefille, a dramatist who comes somewhere about eighth in the main list of her loves, and one 'whose happiness is sacred to me'. To say that she was a mass of contradictions and a most brilliant self-deceiver would be a masterpiece of understatement. What she writes is therefore very unreliable, yet despite her faults she was not without virtues and kindness, for otherwise it is unlikely that the love and friendship between Chopin and herself would have lasted for eight or nine years.

Finally it was all arranged: George Sand, her two children, Maurice and Solange, and a maidservant left Paris on October 18 1838. After stopping at Lyons, Avignon and Arles, they reached Perpignan on October 29. Few people knew that she had left, and Chopin told only three of his closest friends, Fontana, Grzymala, Matuszyński and also Pleyel, that he intended to join her. Chopin asked Fontana to post all his letters in Paris, particularly those to his family. In order to have enough money for this venture, Chopin sold the Preludes (as yet unfinished) for two thousand francs to Pleyel, who paid him five hundred francs in advance, and borrowed another thousand francs from the banker Leo.

35

Chopin left for Perpignan a few days later, accompanied by the Spanish statesman Mendizabal, a friend of George Sand's. He took with him some of Bach's scores, the Preludes on which he was working, and a quantity of music paper, pens and ink. He arrived, as George Sand said, 'fresh as a rose, and rosy as a turnip; looking well besides, having borne his four nights in the mail coach heroically! '. They left in the *Phénician* from Port Vendres and sailed to Barcelona, where they embarked on *El Mallorquin* for Palma, the capital of Majorca. The sea was calm and the voyage was made on a warm night, with the steersman singing softly to keep himself awake. Chopin appears to have been enamoured of the strange character of the rhythms and modulations, which were probably Eastern. The crossing took them about twelve hours.

MAJORCAN ORDEAL

When they arrived in Palma and found that there were no inns or hotels, they had to live for the first week in two scantily furnished rooms in a boarding house in the Calle de la Marina, where the food was almost uneatable.

After a few days George Sand found a house in Establiments near Palma called 'Son-vent'. This house was adequate as long as the weather remained fine, but unfortunately it soon began to pour with rain, and the plaster walls swelled up like sponges. Inside the house, the cold became so intense that they needed fires in order to keep warm and to get dry, in spite of a temperature of eighteen degrees centigrade outside. The fires were nothing more than braziers of charcoal, which smoked because the house was devoid of chimneys, and this greatly aggravated the bronchial cough which Chopin had developed. Two or three days before the rain, they had all gone out for a long walk, which had completely exhausted Chopin, and acute bronchitis set in. Three doctors came to see him and, as he says, 'One sniffed at what I spat up, the second tapped where I spat it from, the third poked about and listened how I spat it. One said that I had died, the second that I am dying, the third that

36

I shall die. And today I am the same as ever.' It has been suggested that this unfortunate walk resulted in the outset of the pulmonary disease which was to kill him eleven years later.

As a result of Chopin's illness, they were asked to leave the house, but not before they had paid for it to be replastered and whitewashed, and bought all the household linen they had used. The Majorcans were terrified of infection. Fortunately, six miles away, at Valdemosa, was the Carthusian monastery which George Sand had discovered, and the French consul gave them hospitality until they could move into it. They were able to buy furniture and to use the cell of a Spanish refugee, which consisted of several rooms. Before he left Paris, Chopin had instructed Pleyel to send him a small upright piano, but it had not yet arrived and all that he had to work on was a poor Spanish instrument, which he had hired. At first he had been tremendously enthusiastic about Majorca: 'I am in Palma, among palms, cedars, cacti, olives, pomegranates, etc. Everything the *Jardin des Plantes* has in its greenhouses. A sky like turquoise, a sea like lapis lazuli, mountains like emerald, air like heaven. Sun all day and hot; everyone in summer clothing; at night, guitars and singing for hours.' However, his mood quickly changed after the rain set in and he became ill. The Pleyel piano did not arrive, nor did any letters: 'The most irregular post on earth', he wrote to Fontana.

George Sand soon found that she had a very difficult and trying patient on her hands. It certainly brought out the best in her. As a mother she was often misguided, but she had a kind heart and was also a very good nurse, doing everything she could to alleviate Chopin's condition. During all the time she knew him she tried to get him to eat properly, to go to bed early, and generally to look after himself. On this score alone, the world owes her a debt of gratitude. Chopin had never been robust, and was prone to persistent bouts of influenza, coughing and bronchitis, but with her careful nursing he was able to throw them off.

Immediately after Chopin died, Grzymala wrote a letter to Leo the banker and said: 'If he [Chopin] had not had the ill luck to know George Sand, who poisoned his whole life, he

37

might have lived to be as old as Cherubini! '. This is only half true and rather harsh. But on the debit side, Chopin would not have spent the disastrous winter in Majorca which undoubtedly undermined his already precarious health. He would not have had to suffer being cast aside and finally rejected in the most callous way when George Sand became tired of him. Nohant should be added to the credit side, for he would not have had this country home had it not been for her.

However, it would be wrong to suppose that Chopin would not have composed some of his greatest works had he not enjoyed the peace and quiet of Nohant. As to George Sand's direct influence on his work, it is not possible to be dogmatic, but as he was musically so self-sufficient it is unlikely that she had any at all. She certainly did not fully understand or appreciate his work, or she could not have made the cardinal blunder of suggesting that the day would come when his music would be orchestrated. It was her artistic circle which, however indirectly, was helpful to the composer.

Eventually, at the end of December, the Pleyel upright piano arrived, but Chopin was forced to pay an exorbitant fee to the customs before they would release it. As soon as he was well enough, he continued working on the Preludes. Five of them, nos 1, 2, 4, 10 and 21—were written in Majorca. The second Prelude is music of unrelieved gloom, perhaps a portrayal of his feelings there when conditions seemed hopeless. The fourth is sad and introspective, but the other three seem less subjective. Chopin became very anxious to finish the Preludes and to send them off to Pleyel, which he did on January 22 1839.

An improvement in Chopin's health was not maintained, and he became extremely impatient to get away. He hated the peasants because they were terrified of his illness, and they looked upon him as a heathen who would end up in hell because be did not go to confession. They even declared that they would refuse to bury him in consecrated ground if he should die, and that no one would give up any ground for his body. They were, of course, very primitive people, but such troubles only aggravated Chopin's already lacerated nerves. He

38

was trapped there by his illness and by the weather, which was
too bad for boats to make the crossing. With the advent of
spring, George Sand said he was beside himself with impatience
to leave.

They had a nightmare journey from Valdemosa to Palma,
since no one would provide a carriage for fear of its being in-
fected, and so poor Chopin had to travel in an open cart, which
proved to be most exhausting. When he arrived in Palma, he
had a very bad haemorrhage of the lungs. At 3 pm on February
13 they left Palma for Barcelona, on a boat with a hundred pigs
on board. The captain would only allow him to sleep in the
worst cabin, because the mattress would have to be burned afterwards. By the time they reached Barcelona Chopin had lost
a great deal of blood and was extremely ill. George Sand sent
a note to the commandant of a French ship stationed there and
a French doctor managed to stop the haemorrhage. The French
consul arranged for them to say in a small village outside Barcelona for a week, after which they set sail again in the *Phéni-
cien*, this time for Marseilles, and now the captain gave up his
cabin to Chopin.

REFUGE AT MARSEILLES

On February 25 the party arrived at Marseilles, where they
stayed for two months, in order to give Chopin time to conva-
lesce. Here, fortunately, George Sand knew Dr Cauvières, who
attended Chopin and said that although his health was seriously
impaired, he might, with care, live for a long time. Dr Cauvières
insisted, however, that he should stay in the south until the
summer. They lodged in the Hôtel de Beauvau, but neither
of them particularly cared for Marseilles, as it was a commercial
port. Moreover, during March, the mistral blew, and they had
to surround themselves with screens in the middle of their
rooms. But Chopin's strength began to return quite quickly,
though he was often overcome by sleep. He began writing to
Fontana about the sale of his compositions, and his tenacity is

reflected in his dealings with his publishers, of whom he had an innate distrust. In those days, compositions were bought outright and no royalties were paid. It is easy, therefore, to understand Chopin's insistence on getting as good a price as he possibly could.

In May, he was so much better that they made an expedition to Italy, going by boat to Genoa, which was unwise, as he was in no condition to visit picture galleries and palaces. On the return journey, when the sea was rough, he became very seasick. After having spent a few days with Dr Cauvières so that Chopin might recover, they set off for Nohant, which he had not yet seen. George Sand had her own carriage sent to meet them at Arles.

FIRST VISIT TO NOHANT

The Château de Nohant Vicq is a house of great charm and character, somewhat English in style and set in a pretty garden. The entrance is opposite the small, old church, which is in the centre of the tiny village. The large, rather Parisian iron gates enclose a circular drive-way with the coach-house set on the left, at right angles to the house. The coach-house still has two carriages in it, and on the other side of the drive grows a very large catalpa tree. Obviously, most of the trees now standing in the garden have grown to their present size during the last one hundred and thirty years, but some were there probably in Chopin's time. One original feature, the round pond, can still be seen. The house, grey stucco outside, is plain and unadorned except by shutters, but is of pleasing proportions. Of all the surviving places connected with Chopin, perhaps Nohant is the least changed. It is true that Chopin's bedroom, which was where he had his piano, and worked, has now been divided into two smaller rooms; but downstairs, the entrance hall, with the fine curving stone staircase, the dining room and the salon are still very much as he knew them.

Chopin was enraptured with Nohant when he first saw it in June 1839, and described it thus to Grzymala: 'Here we are after a week's travelling [from Marseilles]. We arrived very comfortably. The countryside is beautiful: nightingales, skylarks ...'

After about five weeks, Chopin began to get somewhat restive and was anxious to see some of his Polish friends again; he was longing to be back in Paris after an absence of nine months. Nevertheless, he settled down to work, and during the summer produced the first movement, scherzo and finale of the Funeral March Sonata op 35. This is one of the few works that Chopin himself describes. He says of the finale that the two hands are in unison, gossiping after the march. It is a strange enigmatic piece, quite timeless in style.

At the request of Ignaz Moscheles, Chopin also wrote the 'Trois nouvelles Etudes'. They were published in the *Méthode des méthodes de Moscheles et Fétis* in 1840 without opus number, and not posthumously as has been so often stated. He also corrected a Paris edition of the Bach 'Forty-Eight' for himself. He wrote to Fontana thus: [There are] 'engravers' mistakes but also mistakes hallowed by those who are supposed to understand Bach (I have no pretentions to understand better but I do think sometimes I can guess). There, you see, I have boasted to you.'

Towards the end of the summer both Chopin and George Sand were making plans to return to Paris, but decided that they would not live in the same house. There are endless letters of instruction from Chopin to his long-suffering friends Grzymala and Fontana about what kind of house or apartment to look for and how it was to be decorated. Clothes must be ordered and ready for him by the time he arrived.

RETURN TO PARIS

At the beginning of October 1839 they returned, he to 5 Rue Tronchet (which is behind the Madeleine and comprised two rooms with an entrance hall) and she to 16 Rue Pigalle—two separate small houses at the end of a garden, described as 'a little enclosure in the heart of Paris'.

41

Eventually, in October 1841, after less than two years in Rue Tronchet, Chopin moved to the smaller of the two houses in Rue Pigalle which George Sand had taken. After living *en famille* for the best part of a year he missed family life. He also found Rue Tronchet too cold and too far from Rue Pigalle. He gave up Rue Tronchet to Matuszyński on the understanding that he himself could have a room there if he came to Paris on his own, presumably from Nohant. Chopin occupied the lower ground floor of the small house in Rue Pigalle and Maurice Sand had his room upstairs. They all met for meals, either in Chopin's rooms or in George Sand's.

His pupils flocked back to him and he led a very busy and full life. He met the pianist Moscheles, who had for long sought his acquaintance, and the two played at court together. Moscheles has left a most interesting account of this occasion, mentioning that Chopin was a great favourite of the royal family. At the beginning of 1840 George Sand's financial position was bad, and so for this year they decided not to got to Nohant; because as she entertained lavishly there, it usually proved to be much more expensive than staying quietly in Paris. 'Chopin gives five lessons every day, and I write eight or ten pages every night', she wrote. In the summer they each left Paris on different occasions to stay with friends for short visits.

During 1840 Chopin published eight works, including the second Ballade, the third Scherzo, the second Impromptu and the Waltz in A flat op 42. He continued to have a certain amount of trouble either with Breitkopf & Härtel or their agent in Paris, Probst, as can be seen from a letter he wrote to Breitkopf on December 14 1839, threatening to break off relations because they had failed to reply to him. The Countess d'Agoult put a false construction on the situation between Chopin and Breitkopf. She had become jealous of the relationship between Chopin and George Sand and never lost an opportunity to behave unpleasantly, at first behind their backs. She wrote to Liszt telling him that Breitkopf had instructed Probst not to buy any more of Chopin's works except at a low price, as nobody was buying them in Germany. Obviously she had heard that Chopin wanted to raise his prices, and that he also needed a loan of 150 francs. According to her, Probst was forced to tell Chopin these 'facts' from Breitkopf, although he wished, she says, to spare Chopin's feelings. Judging from Chopin's next letter to Breitkopf and the fact that they continued to publish everything he sent them, it was pure fabrication on the part of the Countess.

CONCERT AT THE SALLE PLEYEL

On April 26 1841 Chopin gave a concert at the Salle Pleyel, his first in Paris for three years. The relevant correspondence between Marie d'Agoult and Liszt at this time is singularly unpleasant and vindictive, particularly about this concert. Ernest Legouvé had been requested by the *Gazette musicale* to review it, but Liszt asked that he might be allowed to write instead. Chopin was not particularly pleased at this. Legouvé told Chopin that he should be, as Liszt would make a 'fine kingdom for you'; Chopin replied, 'Yes, in his empire'. It is true that the notice stresses the social rather than the musical side of the concert, but whether this is enough to justify the suggestion that the Countess d'Agoult wrote it for Liszt is another matter. Since to the Princess von Sayn-Wittgenstein falls the doubtful credit of writing most of Liszt's biography of Chopin, Liszt may well have allowed himself to be influenced by the Countess.

The worthwhile notice of this concert appeared in *La France musicale*, where Chopin is compared with Schubert: 'One has done for the pianoforte what the other has done for the voice . . . One can say that he is the creator of a school of playing and of a school of composition. Nothing, in truth, equals the lightness and sweetness of his [playing], nothing can be found to compare with his works in originality, distinction and grace. Chopin is a pianist apart, who should not be and cannot be compared with anyone.'

George Sand's letter of April 18 1841 to the singer Pauline Viardot, then in London, gives us a very clear and vivid picture of the ordinary human side of Chopin, and also makes amusing reading: ' . . . A great astounding piece of news is that little Chip-Chip is to give a Grrrrand Concert. His friends have plagued him so much that he has given in . . . he imagined that it would be so difficult to arrange that he would have to give it up. But things moved more quickly than he bargained for. Scarcely had he uttered the fatal *yes* than everything was settled as if by a miracle. Three-quarters of the tickets had gone before any announcement was made. Then he woke up as if from a dream; and there is no more amusing sight than our meticulous and irresolute Chip-Chip compelled to keep his promise. He hoped you would come and sing for him. When I received your letter destroying his hopes, he wanted to put off his concert. But it couldn't be done—he had gone too far. . . . This Chopinesque nightmare will take place at Pleyel's rooms on the 26th. He will have nothing to do with posters or programmes and does not want a large audience. He wants to have the affair kept quiet. So many things alarm him that I suggest that he should play without candles or audience and on a dumb keyboard . . .'

Later, when she herself had to lecture in public, she remembered Chopin and was more sympathetic. He played the F major Ballade, the C sharp minor Scherzo, four Mazurkas op 41, and the A major Polonaise op 40.

SUMMER AT NOHANT

At the end of May or beginning of June, Chopin and the Sand ménage set off for Nohant, to which they had been looking forward after an absence of eighteen months. Chopin's letters from Nohant at this time reveal how he settled down there, but also how he was constantly asking Fontana to purchase various things for him in Paris, pay his bills, copy out the latest works he had written, or send him other works such as Cherubini's *Treatise on counterpoint*. There is one letter written from Nohant on Sunday June 20 1841, in which he gives copious instructions and directions and sketches of where to go, where to find something, what it looks like, and after all this, finishes: 'Never mind it, Dear –, I have thought it over. If I need it I'll write to you.' It reads not unlike E M Delafield's *Diary of a provincial lady.*

However, he could be very business-like when he chose, as letters to his publishers show. He was particular, too, about the condition of his piano. He wrote to Pleyel from Nohant asking him for a better one, 'for mine is not good', and a new one was sent by express: 'What sort of voice the piano has, I don't know yet, as it is not unpacked. The great event is tomorrow.' He thanked Pleyel, saying, 'I have not played on it much as the weather is so fine that I am out of doors nearly all the time'. To Fontana he wrote, 'Don't tell Pleyel that he has sent me a very bad piano'.

Mlle de Rozières, who was a pupil of Chopin and a friend of George Sand, had been asked by the latter to teach the piano to her daughter, Solange. Mlle de Rozières had become attracted to Maria Wodzińska's brother Anton, and Chopin was not pleased that she should have learned of his previous engagement to Maria and, in all probability, discussed it with George Sand. He became very irritated about the whole business, and even spent one day without saying a word to anyone. He was also annoyed to learn at this time that Haslinger in Vienna had printed the Sonata op 4 and the 'Swiss Boy' Variations, and wanted to publish them now that Chopin had become well-known. He refused to correct the proofs and the works were not issued until after his death.

It is interesting that during the last week in September Chopin was prepared to make the journey from Nohant to Paris, a distance of 165 miles, just for a few days. This entailed sitting up in a coach all night. He went to look at apartments, for, as already mentioned, he wanted to move out of 5 Rue Tronchet. By a strange coincidence he considered one in the Place Vendôme, to which he moved almost exactly eight years later. He even looked at another apartment in Rue Tronchet before he finally decided to move to 16 Rue Pigalle.

In his letters to Fontana, written during this summer and autumn, there are numerous references to various publishers

45

and how Fontana should deal with them. Chopin was most emphatic about how much money should be asked for different works: 'When you see my manuscripts with their tiny notes (like fly-marks) you yourself will agree I have the right to ask 600 [francs].'

Fontana's name should have been factotum, because he was expected to make copies (sometimes three of one work) of the new compositions Chopin sent him. This was done in order to send them to Breitkopf in Germany, to various publishers in Paris, and to Wessel in London, since simultaneous publication was required by law. Chopin was extremely angry with Wessel for giving his pieces 'silly titles', in spite of his express orders to the contrary. He considered that this was why Wessel lost money on them. He begged Fontana not to tear or crumple his manuscripts, but to be careful of them, as he was so pleased with all his hard work, adding that he would go mad if he had to copy out 'those eighteen pages' again.

A curiously interesting and revealing paragraph comes in another letter to Fontana written on October 20: 'Today I have finished the Fantasia [op 49]—and the weather is lovely, but I am sad at heart—not that it matters. If it were otherwise, my existence would perhaps be of no use to anyone. Let us save ourselves up for life after death—NB, not in Leroux's conception—according to him, the younger a man commits suicide, the wiser he is. Don't deduce any wrong ideas from that—I'm just going to dinner.'

Chopin was back in Paris by November 1 and a month later he played at court. In a letter from George Sand to her half-brother Hippolyte Chatiron, we read that he wore a white tie and was not too pleased about it. Presumably he disliked having to wear full evening, or court dress. In this same letter George Sand also said that some of his pupils protested that the Rue Pigalle was too far from their 'elegant districts'. Chopin replied to them: 'I give much better lessons in my own room and on my own piano for twenty francs than I do for thirty francs at my pupils' homes, and besides, you have to send your carriages to fetch me.' Several chose to come to him; others

46

paid thirty francs (the equivalent today of twenty-five to thirty pounds) and sent their carriages. It was George Sand who suggested this and who had considerable trouble in getting him to agree to it: 'With his poor health he must earn money at a high rate so as to be able to work less. Anyhow, he is quite well now and so am I.'

In February 1842 Chopin gave another concert at Pleyel's, which was even more brilliant than that of 1841, before one of the most distinguished audiences ever seen in Paris. Viardot sang, accompanied by Chopin, and the 'cellist Franchomme played. The programme included the A flat Ballade, three Mazurkas, four Nocturnes, among them op 48 no 2, the Prelude in D flat and the Impromptu op 51. In March he was not well, and the sudden death of his great friend Jan Matuszynski in April caused a severe setback. George Sand was anxious that they should leave for Nohant as soon as possible, where she felt his health would recover more quickly.

WITH FRIENDS AND FAMILY IN NOHANT AND PARIS

Eugène Delacroix visited Nohant at the beginning of June 1842. Both he and Chopin had a great regard for one another and shared a love of Mozart's operas. Delacroix, too, was consumptive and in many ways not unlike Chopin. He was immensely appreciative of Chopin's music and playing. According to George Sand, Chopin, while equally appreciating Delacroix as a man, did not value him as an artist. This is hard to understand and it is perhaps worthwhile pointing out that it is *only* George Sand who said this. There is no doubt that she considered herself, in many ways, superior to Chopin and at times became jealous of him. She made deprecating remarks about him, his likes and dislikes; the one quoted above about Delacroix is an example.

Some of this censoriousness may have originated in fun, but not always, and she was by no means always right in her judgement of Chopin. Before Delacroix arrived he wrote to George

47

Sand: 'Tell my dear little Chopin that the only kind of entertainment I love is to stroll along garden walks talking about music, and listening to it in the evening on a sofa, when God takes possession of his divine fingers'.

Delacroix wrote to a friend about Nohant: 'The place is very pleasant, and the hosts could not be kinder or more considerate . . . From time to time you hear through the window which opens on to the garden, wafts of Chopin's music, as he works in his own room; this blends with the song of the nightingales and the scent of roses . . . I have endless tête-à-têtes with Chopin, of whom I am very fond, and who is a man of rare distinction: the truest artist I have ever met. He is one of the very few people one can admire and respect.'

After Delacroix returned to Paris he wrote to George Sand, thanking her and saying, 'Take care of yourself then, take care of Chopin. Perhaps he will work now that I don't interrupt him so often; I am sure he neglected his work on several occasions to keep me company.'

By this time Chopin began to look upon Nohant as the place where he could compose. Since George Sand was industrious herself, the atmosphere would have helped him to work. She said that he always longed for Nohant, but that almost as soon as he got there, wanted to be back in Paris, and that he hated the country. He could be critical of it if the weather were bad, and said in a letter to Fontana, 'It's all mud and rain here'. At Nohant, he would have had more time to compose and fewer interruptions than in Paris where he was busy teaching. This is not to suggest, of course, that he turned off his inspiration the moment he returned to Paris, or that he could even have done so if he wished; sometimes he cancelled lessons, either to finish a work or to write one out.

Chopin and George Sand returned to Paris in July to look for new apartments; they had decided that they needed bigger rooms, as those in the two houses in Rue Pigalle were very small. They were lucky to find both nos 9 and 5 in the Place d'Orléans, which were in opposite corners of a tiny square. So they returned to Nohant, staying there until they moved into

48

their new abodes in October 1842. Madame Marliani, a friend of George Sand, lived at no 7 'between our two', George Sand wrote. She went on: 'We had only to cross a large sanded court with plants in it, which was always well kept, in order to meet, sometimes in her apartment, sometimes in mine, sometimes in Chopin's, when he was in the mood to make music. We all dined together with her, sharing the expense . . . Chopin was glad to have a fine separate drawing-room to which he could retire to compose or dream. But he was fond of society, and hardly availed himself of his room except for giving lessons. It was only at Nohant that he created and wrote.' (The last sentence is not entirely true, as can be seen from the chronological index of his works.)

Sometimes Chopin would open the long windows in the evening and play, and the little square was filled with his music. Next June, 1843, when they were at Nohant again, George Sand and Chopin went for long outings, he riding on his donkey and she walking. In October he wrote to Auguste Leo that he had just returned from a few days' excursion along the banks of the Creuse, 'very picturesque but rather tiring'. He again climbed everywhere on his donkey and slept on straw.

Chopin returned to Paris before George Sand at the end of October 1843. She wrote to Carlotta Marliani: 'Here comes my little Chopin. Do take care of him whatever he says. His daily routine goes to pieces when I am not there. He has a man-servant who is alright but is stupid. I am not worried about his dinners because he will be invited out on all sides. But in the morning, in the rush of his lessons, I am afraid he will forget to swallow a cup of drinking chocolate or clear soup. When I am there I make him have it . . . His Polish servant can quite well cook him a little casserole or a cutlet. . . Do let me know if Chopin is at all unwell, for I would leave everything and go and look after him.' George Sand also wrote in the same vein to Mlle de Rozières, and told her to send for Dr Molin, the homoeopath who looked after him better than anyone else when he was ill. It was extremely sad that George Sand was unable to sustain her affection for Chopin when he became less well and thus more difficult.

49

The next year Chopin was prostrated by the death of his father, Nicholas Chopin, on May 3 1844, and became very ill for a few weeks. George Sand wrote: 'He was visibly wasting away, and I did not know what medicines to use to combat the increasing nervous irritation.' When his family heard how ill he had become, it was decided that Louise and her husband Kalasanty Jedrzejewicz should come to see him. In the meantime George Sand took him to Nohant and wrote to Louise: 'You will find my dear child very thin and changed since you last saw him, but do not be too alarmed about his health. There has been little change in his general condition for the last six years, during which time I have seen him every day. A rather violent fit of coughing every morning, two or three more serious attacks every winter, lasting only two or three days, sometimes neuralgia, this is his usual condition. For the rest, his chest is healthy and there is no injury to his delicate physique. I always hope that in time he will become stronger, but I am sure that with a regular life and care, his health will last as long as that of anyone else;'

Louise and her husband arrived at Nohant at the beginning of August 1844 and stayed for a month. Chopin returned with them to Paris for a few days, taking them to see the actress Rachel (stage-name of Élisa Félix). Just how much the visit meant to Chopin can be seen from a letter he wrote to Louise after he had returned to Nohant: 'Often when I come in, I look to see if there is nothing left of you and I see only the same place by the couch, where we drank our chocolate. More of you has remained in my room—there is a piece of your embroidery work on the table for that little slipper, folded inside an English blotter,—and on the piano a tiny pencil, which was in your little purse, and which I find most useful.'

CREATIVE WORK AND DAILY LIFE

During the summer and autumn of 1844 he worked on the Sonata in B minor op 58, which is one of his greatest works. For many decades it was not appreciated or understood, and it has come in for some silly and pointless censure, which can be found in some of the books discussed in the next section of this book. Chopin was always extremely critical of his own music and compelled himself to rework and polish it into its final form. He would keep his compositions by him for some time, in order to judge them more objectively before letting a publisher have them.

The fact that in the autumn of the following year he began the Sonata for 'cello and piano op 65 certainly suggests that he was satisfied with op 58. Chopin had always been attracted to the 'cello, and his friendship with Auguste Franchomme doubtless encouraged and inspired him to write this sonata. Franchomme did, in fact, help and advise Chopin about the 'cello part. Both op 58 and op 65 show Chopin's mastery of sonata form in large-scale works, and prove his ability to achieve sustained inspiration. After Fontana left for America, Franchomme became embroiled in dealings with Chopin's publishers when Grzymala was ill, or when Chopin felt it politic to give him a rest! It was an unenviable task.

Chopin paid a second visit to Paris from Nohant on September 23 1844 in order to see his publisher and Franchomme. He wrote to George Sand that he had been to see Delacroix, who was ill: 'We talked for two and a half hours; of music, of painting, and especially of you'. He finally returned to Paris, before George Sand, on November 27 and in December wrote to her rather poetically: 'It has been snowing since yesterday morning . . . your little garden is covered in snowballs, sugar, swansdown, cream cheese, white as Solange's hands and Maurice's teeth'; and to Marie de Rozières he wrote during this winter: 'I do not think I can go out as it is so slippery'. During the unusually early and bitterly cold winter of 1844-45, Chopin's health grew worse. Even the following Easter, 1845, he wrote that it was colder than ever. George Sand was disturbed by his condition.

In two letters written to his family from Nohant in July and October 1845, one catches glimpses of Chopin that give an idea of what his everyday life was like, what he thought about various things, what interested, amused or irritated him. That

51

summer was very wet, and after mentioning the storms he says: 'I was not made for the country, though fresh air is good for me. I don't play much as my piano is out of tune . . . I feel strange here this year [ie without his sister]; often in the morning I go into the next room, but there's no one there. Sometimes I seem to fill the place of an acquaintance who comes for a few days.' Here are the first distant rumblings of the approaching domestic catastrophe. He went on: ' . . . so I do not drink chocolate in the morning, and have moved my piano; it is by the wall where the little sofa . . . used to be. The bureau at which I write stands in the middle . . . on the right Cherubini; in front of me that repeater you sent me, in its case (it's four o'clock); roses and pinks, pens . . . I am always with one foot among you.'

'I am just back from a drive with Sol, who took me all over the place in a cabriolet in the company of Jacques. Jacques is an enormous dog . . . who is to replace old Simon who has aged greatly this year and has a paralysed paw . . . When it rains, Jacques squeezes himself into the cabriolet and lies down; but however carefully he disposes himself, his head gets wet on one side and his tail on the other; he tries to take shelter, but he is too big . . .'

Sometime during December 1845 he tried to persuade his mother to come and stay with him. She thought she might visit Paris with some friends, and wrote: 'I would have to stay with you the whole winter, and you, poor boy, what would you do with me? I should only be a source of worry to you. I know your good nature: you would always be uneasy about me, you would feel I was bored, not comfortable . . . No, my dear, I won't do it.'

Earlier, he had written to his family: 'I should like now to finish my violoncello sonata, barcarolle and something else that I don't know how to name . . . [the Polonaise-Fantasie op 61] . . . I have tried over part of my violoncello sonata with Franchomme, and it goes well.' It was in the last letter to his family from Nohant (written in October 1846) that he said: 'Sometimes I am satisfied with my violoncello sonata, sometimes not. I throw it into the corner then take it up again.'

During the spring of 1846 George Sand wrote to Louise and put forward her plan of taking Chopin to the south of France to avoid the worst of the winter; she felt he would get rid of his cough if he could escape from the cold for a whole year. She also had an estimate from a firm in Paris for putting central heating in at Nohant, mainly for Chopin's benefit in the spring and autumn. Before George Sand left for Nohant, he gave a party for her. 'Music, flowers and food' were the three words printed on the invitations. Delacroix and Pauline Viardot were present at the distinguished gathering.

THE LAST VISIT TO NOHANT

A few weeks after the party, Chopin set out for Nohant, not knowing it was to be his last visit. He found it hard to work there during that final summer. He told Franchomme he was doing his best, but he was stuck: 'If it goes on like that, my new works will give neither the impression of warbling birds, nor even broken china'.

Maurice, Solange and Augustine Brault (whom George Sand adopted in 1846, and who was the daughter of her cousin Adèle Brault) contributed more than anything else to the changed atmosphere at Nohant. They found fault with the old servants, who were all replaced by 1847; they were uncomplimentary about any Polish friends of Chopin's. This is why, in the following year, before the real trouble at Nohant started, Chopin began to wish that he was not going there. In 1846 Delacroix was at Nohant again and spoke of Chopin playing Beethoven divinely. George Sand said, 'the household makes light of everything but not of Chopin'. Maurice was very jealous of him and succeeded in getting his mother to listen to his own point of view and to disregard Chopin's. Once he also took it upon himself to try to put Chopin in his place, which made the latter furiously angry, and to make matters worse, George Sand took her son's part.

In June 1846 she began publishing her novel *Lucrezia Floriani*. It was issued as a serial and, as she had so often done in the past, she read it aloud to Chopin. In spite of her denials, it was obvious to all that Prince Karol, a distinguished neurasthenic, was a portrait of the composer; she herself was less well drawn as Lucrezia. The book describes actual incidents that took place at Nohant. No one knows whether Chopin recognised himself at first, but later on, none of his friends left him in any doubt whatsoever. It was not, however, the cause of the rupture.

Solange became engaged to marry Fernand de Préaulx, who lived near Nohant, but when she went to Paris to sign a marriage contract, she suddenly refused, as she had been attracted by a sculptor named Jean Baptiste Clésinger. George Sand took her back to Nohant, but Clésinger followed them there, seduced her and tried to carry her off. Not even Maurice knew of this. Chopin had liked and approved of Préaulx but he did not care for Clésinger, who had a very bad reputation. He also knew that Solange had really wanted to marry Victor de Laprade, a poet, but the latter's family would not allow it. Chopin considered that George Sand should have tried to help Solange to get over this disappointment and not to have allowed the marriage with Clésinger.

THE BONDS ARE BROKEN

In April and May of 1847 Chopin was extremely ill with a violent attack of asthma, and if he had been invited to Solange's wedding, which was at Nohant, he would have been unable to go, but he was kept in the dark about the whole thing. After the honeymoon, Solange and Clésinger returned to Nohant; Clésinger at once fell out with Maurice, and Solange ruined Augustine's chances of marriage with a friend of Maurice's, Théodore Rousseau, by telling him that Augustine had been Maurice's mistress. Solange also accused her mother of an amorous affair with Victor Borie, another of Maurice's friends.

54

There ensued a violent scene and Maurice would have shot Clésinger if George Sand had not rushed between them. The Clésingers were then turned out of the house.

Solange wrote to Chopin an untrue account of what happened and asked him to lend her his carriage as she was ill. Chopin innocently replied: 'I am most grieved to hear that you are ill. I hasten to place my carriage at your service. I have written to this effect to your mother.' It was this letter from him that made George Sand write to him in the unprecedented way that she did. Though her letter has not survived, Chopin showed it to Delacroix, who described it as 'atrocious'.

There is no doubt that fundamentally George Sand was tired of Chopin, but it is not true to say, as she did, that his love for her was dead. Whether she consciously seized upon the idea of forbidding him to mention Solange, or to have anything to do with her if he came to Nohant for that fateful summer, it is difficult to say. She must have known that he would not allow her to dictate to him in this way, and also that, by so doing, she was bound to damage their relationship. Nevertheless, her mood is understandable at the time when she wrote to Chopin. She felt, quite mistakenly, that he was betraying her in taking Solange's part, although she did not approve of Clésinger any more than he did. She knew also that Solange had slandered her and was doing her best to poison Chopin's mind against her.

Undoubtedly Maurice's reaction to Chopin's illness and his influence on his mother contributed much to George Sand's change of heart. Besides Solange's determination to get Chopin on her side against her mother, it only needed the weakness in George Sand's character to achieve the upper hand for the relationship to be broken. One thing is certain: George Sand could never have foreseen that Chopin's last letter to her would so effectively undo all the self-vindication she indulged in. His letter is a model of tact and tenderness. She had tried to make out that Chopin was completely incapable of understanding human nature on any point, and that he had never faced realities. She could not allow him to act as head of her household. She seized upon his irritability, which was due to his increasing ill-health and aggravated by the bad behaviour of her children, as the reason for her turning against him. In all this she was utterly dishonest and irresponsible. Chopin would have made a vastly better and more balanced head of a family than she ever managed to be. But he never sought this position, and wished only to give the help and advice which he saw she so desperately needed. Chopin was right when he said later that her treatment of Solange would have been forgivable in a woman of twenty, but not in one of forty. It should be remembered that by this time Solange was nearly nineteen and Maurice was twenty-four. They were no longer children, and it was a great pity that George Sand seemed unable to realise this.

In a letter to his family, written the following Christmas, one sentence stands out: 'One might imagine she wanted to get rid of both her daughter and myself at one stroke because we were in the way'. In spite of the wicked lies Solange told Chopin about her mother, the remark is nevertheless true, because later, when mutual friends left George Sand in no doubt as to Chopin's real feelings for her, she made all manner of weak excuses for not seeing him. The two met once more, accidentally, in Paris the following year.

George Sand's description of this meeting is obviously an appalling lie. She said he avoided her, and when she sent someone after him, he came back unwillingly and showed in his attitude and looks an anger verging on hatred. Chopin would have no reason to paint a false picture of the meeting for Solange's benefit. He asked George Sand if she had had any news of Solange, to which she replied, 'a week ago'. He told her that she had become a grandmother and that Solange had a daughter, adding that he was very glad to be the first to give her this news. He bowed and went downstairs. He realised that he had forgotten to say that Solange was doing well, so he sent the friend who was with him to tell her as he was unable to manage the stairs again. George Sand came down herself and asked him all sorts of questions about Solange, which Chopin answered quite naturally. She ended by asking him how he was. He replied that he was well and asked the concierge to open the door: 'I bowed, and found myself in the Square d'Orléans on foot . . .' One of the saddest things about the break with George Sand is that, apart from shortening his life, it caused him to lose the will, but not altogether the desire, to compose.

The Violoncello Sonata op 65 was published in 1847 and was the last work to appear during Chopin's lifetime; apart from a few short Mazurkas and a song, he composed nothing more. On February 16 1848 he gave what proved to be his last concert in Paris. Pleyel decorated the stairs and the hall with flowers to make him feel at home and more willing to play, as Chopin wrote in a letter to his family. Tickets cost twenty francs each and there were only three hundred seats. It was six years since Chopin had played in public, and the tickets were all sold two weeks beforehand. Nevertheless, he was astonished by such eagerness and thought that he was playing 'worse now than ever before'. The critics, however, did not think so and the long notice published in the *Gazette musicale* makes it clear that Chopin's artistry and musicianship still defied description and were things apart.

TRIBULATIONS IN LONDON AND SCOTLAND

A week after the concert, the revolution of 1848 broke out in Paris. A second concert was cancelled and many of Chopin's pupils left the city. One of them, Jane Wilhelmina Stirling, gave him a very pressing invitation to return with her to England, and he accepted it. He arrived in London on April 20 and was immediately taken up by fashionable society. This greatly taxed his strength. He was invited by the Philharmonic Society to play one of his concertos, but declined when he heard that they had only one rehearsal, which was public. Queen Victoria heard him at Stafford House at a party given by the Duchess of Sutherland. He gave two public matinées, one at 99 Eaton Place, the house of Mrs Sartoris, and the other at Lord Falmouth's, 2 St James's Square. He also did a little teaching, mainly of society ladies, who wished to be able to say that they had studied with him. Jane Stirling and her sister Mrs Erskine (his Scottish ladies, as he called them) gave him no peace; they were very socially minded, and he found most exhausting the three or four hours spent daily in a jolting carriage being dragged around London to pay visits. He wrote, 'It's as if I had travelled from Paris to Boulogne! And the distances here! '

Once the London season was over he went to Scotland, where he was again given little peace. He no sooner became used to one place than he was carried off somewhere else. Many of his letters written from both London and Scotland give a vivid picture of the life he had to lead and of the fashions of the time; he had a remarkably balanced and philosophic outlook. In Edinburgh, Glasgow and Manchester he gave concerts which brought in a little money. This was much needed, because all that he had made in London had been swallowed up by the fashionable apartments he had taken and by the high cost of living.

All the time he was in Britain his health was declining; he was constantly spitting blood and, as he put it, was only half alive. He was exceedingly bored by Jane Stirling and her sister, whom he was unable to shake off. The fact that Jane Stirling was in love with him made it still more trying, because he had good reason to be grateful to her; he frequently said how kind and considerate she was.

While he was staying at Johnstone Castle near Glasgow he narrowly escaped being killed when travelling in a small *coupé*. The horses bolted, but the vehicle was fortunately stopped by a tree from falling over a precipice. Chopin climbed out of the wreck with no worse injury than bruised legs. He stayed at Keir, near Stirling, and headed a letter from there: 'Sunday. No post, no railway, no carriage (even for a drive); not a boat, not even a dog to whistle to! ' At Keir, there is still an Erard piano made in London in 1841 (a poor thing compared with the French ones) on which he played in the evenings after dinner, 'because', as he wrote, 'they usually want to hear me; then my good Daniel carries me up to my bedroom (as you know, that is usually upstairs here), and undresses me, gets me to bed, leaves the light; and I am free to breathe and dream till it is time to begin all over again. And when I get a little bit used to it, then it is time to go somewhere else; for my Scottish ladies give me no peace.'

Chopin arrived back in London again after being nearly killed by kindness in Scotland. At the end of October he had to stay indoors for three weeks suffering from a heavy cold, headaches and shortness of breath. He went to the Guildhall on November 16 to play at a concert and ball given in aid of Polish refugees. It was his last appearance in public. He was by now desperate to return home to Paris, particularly because of the fogs, and he left London on November 23. He had written to Grzymala from London: 'I don't care about anything . . . now my life is so unbearable . . . it would give me relief if I could curse Lucretia. But no doubt she also suffers. But what am I going back for? Why should God kill me this way, not at once, but little by little?' His piano-tuner had drowned himself, his bootmaker had died, and so had Dr Molin, the only doctor in whom he had any faith. Chopin was in utter despair.

FINAL RETURN TO PARIS

No doubt it was a relief to the sufferer to be back amongst his own friends again. He still thought he might recover.

Delacroix visited him; so too, did Delphina Potocka, who sang for him on two occasions; the pianist Alkan also saw him. On April 22 1849 he managed to attend the first performance of Meyerbeer's *Le prophète*, which filled him with horror. His life was almost over now, but there remained the most pathetic struggle with the relentless disease which was to kill him. Chopin had never saved any money, and now that he could no longer compose or earn by teaching to keep himself, he was forced to accept money from his mother and his friends. Jane

59

Stirling had sent him 25,000 francs in March, but owing to a complicated misunderstanding the money did not reach him until the end of July, and then he accepted only 15,000 francs. His doctors felt that he should spend the summer in a quieter and higher neighbourhood, He therefore moved to 74 Rue Chaillot, where he enjoyed more sun, and from his windows could see right over Paris.

Once there, he wrote to Louise telling her how ill he was, and asked her to come to him. She arrived with her husband and daughter on August 9 and, for a little while, this revived him; she nursed him until the end. He had written to Grzymala a month before, saying: 'I see he [the doctor] regards me as consumptive, for he ordered a teaspoonful of something with lichen in it'.

Tytus Woyciechowski, who was in Carlsbad, tried to go and see him, but Russian subjects were not allowed into France without permits. Tytus therefore went to Ostend, but by this time, September 12, Chopin was too ill to travel there, so they never met again. Chopin wrote to Franchomme, who was at Tours, on September 17, and this was the last letter he wrote. A week later he removed to 12 Place Vendôme, the most splendid of all his apartments, where he lived only another three weeks, in a pitiful state.

His great comfort was his sister Louise, and it is sad to learn that her husband Kalasanty was unable to conceal completely his intense jealousy of Chopin. He reproached Chopin for preventing Louise from having enough sleep. Chopin liked to talk late at night and tell Louise all his troubles and what concerned him most. Later on, Louise suffered from her husband's despotism and hatred of anything to do with Chopin.

On October 13 he made his confession and received the last sacraments. Chopin was always very reticent and little is known about his religious views except that he was a Catholic. George Sand said that one might be in his society for a long time without getting to know his religious ideas. It is possible that she undermined his beliefs, as Catholicism seemed to her a childish and deplorable superstition. He is supposed to have said to the priest: 'In order not to offend my mother [who was a devout Catholic] I would not die without receiving the sacraments, but I do not understand them in the way that you desire'. Delphina Potocka saw Chopin again on October 15 and he asked her to sing. In the early hours of the morning of October 17 1849 he died.

The funeral took place at the Madeleine on October 30. Mozart's Requiem was sung, and the funeral march from Chopin's Sonata in B flat minor op 35, orchestrated by Réber was played. There were four thousand people present, and they made their way in a long procession to the Père-Lachaise cemetery, where Chopin was buried. His heart was removed from his body and his sister took it back to Poland.

The urn containing it was placed in a column in the Church of the Holy Cross at Warsaw, where it remains to this day. During the last war, it was removed to a place of safety and afterwards returned. Although the church was largely destroyed in 1944, the column which contained Chopin's heart survived.

Books in English
about Chopin

LETTERS

Chopin's letters paint a vivid self-portrait, for he wrote in a lively and amusing style, often making witty and down-to-earth comments on people and their behaviour. The letters also show that he had a remarkably balanced outlook on life. The earliest publication of some of them forms part of the first serious full length biography to be written, *Frederick Chopin. His life and letters* by Moritz Karasowski, translated by Emily Hill. The first edition appeared in New York in 1878, the next in London (William Reeves 1879, 3rd edition 1938), with additional letters. The text of the letters was distorted and the chronology rather inaccurate.

In the first edition the letters end with Chopin's second visit to Vienna in 1831, because, for some inexplicable reason, Karasowski returned to Chopin's family many of the letters which Chopin wrote to them from Paris. Unfortunately they perished in 1863 when the Russians destroyed all Chopin's possessions still preserved in Warsaw. The only value of the letters used by Karasowski lies in the translation by Emily Hill, which seems near in style to the spirit of the original.

No other English translation appeared for nearly sixty years, but then full amends were made by *Chopin's letters, collected by Henry Opieński, translated from the original Polish and French with a preface and additional notes by E L Voynich*

(NY, Knopf 1931, repr Vienna House, 1972; Desmond Harmsworth 1932). Although later research has altered some of Opieński's chronology, his edition was a remarkable achievement, and the translation is very readable, considering how idiomatic was Chopin's style in both languages. This collection comprises 294 items, including a few diary entries and notes, entirely written by the composer. But this was far from being all the letters and documents relevant to him. The huge task of amassing them was undertaken by Bronislaw Edouard Sydow, to a total of nearly 800; they were published in French in 3 volumes, 1953, 1954 and 1960 respectively, and in Polish in 2 volumes, 1955. Of this total, however, a high proportion consists of visiting cards, memoranda and the like, which are of rather limited interest to the general reader.

Sydow's collection included both letters written to Chopin and others written about him by his contemporaries. From this assemblage, Arthur Hedley produced *Selected correspondence of Fryderyk Chopin* (Heinemann, 1962), 'translated and edited with additional material and a commentary'. It amounts to 348 letters. The idiom of this translation may be rather modern for some tastes, and although the total exceeds that of Voynich's edition, Hedley omitted sections of many of them. For instance, the endings of nine letters which Chopin wrote to Tytus Woyciechowski have been suppressed. Some other letters are left out altogether, but this was due to the publisher's insistence on limiting the space. (There are one or two surprising mistakes in translation.) Hedley includes an appendix on the Potocka letters, which he dismisses as forgeries.

Sydow also made a contribution to *Frederic Chopin*, a symposium edited by Stephen P Mizwa (Macmillan NY, 1949), which is entitled 'Ipse dixit' and is the only significant part of an otherwise unimportant book. It consists of extracts from the letters Chopin is supposed to have written to Delphina Potocka and which Sydow translated and selected. They contain Chopin's comments on music, musicians, music critics, himself and his works, but all the eroticism, which has been the main stumbling block to their publication as authentic, is

63

omitted. Yet what we are left with could be far more damaging to Chopin's reputation than any eroticism. The truisms on music, his own in particular, are completely artificial, even unnatural. The style is laboured and utterly unlike Chopin's known correspondence. It is also inconceivable that Chopin should have written *only* to Delphina Potocka about music. Similar pronouncements would inevitably occur in letters to other people, and they do not.

As to the idea of Chopin writing erotic letters, the reader is referred to George Sand's letter to Grzymala, written in June 1838 about Chopin and sex (quoted on page 14). She also wrote that he was afraid of what people would think. Even in his authentic letters Chopin writes carefully, and is often concerned about what people might say if such and such a thing became known.

Chopin's letters to Delphina Potocka by Matteo Gliński (Windsor, Ontario, 1960) is an unconvincing lecture which attempts to establish authenticity. Although the photographs of the original copies have been found since this lecture was published, not one really convincing fact or argument emerges. The blind determination of the writer to discredit anyone with different opinions serves only to underline the weakness of his hypothesis. Gliński states in the English preface to these letters, which are as yet only available complete in Polish, that 'they can no longer be considered as controversial'. Such a statement is premature and therefore unscholarly. If they are good forgeries one would expect that the writing would 'closely resemble authenticated handwriting of Chopin'. All that has been found are photocopies, which offer no evidence as to the paper or the ink of the originals. Until, however, the originals are found, the subject should not perhaps be regarded as closed.

At the end of *The skein of legends about Chopin* by Adam Harasowski (Glasgow, William Maclellan, 1967), there is an excellent evaluation of the controversy over the Delphina Potocka letters. Harasowski gives the history of them and provides a balanced and objective summary of all the possible theories up to 1967.

BIOGRAPHIES

There are twenty-two biographies published in English about
Chopin. Although he is relatively near us in time and his life
is well documented, the picture which emerges from many of
these books with surprising persistence is frequently inaccurate
and unbalanced. From the outset, Chopin was at the mercy of
the Victorians, who did their utmost to mould him in their own
image, to smother him in first-hand 'reminiscences', usually produced thirty years later. They made him conform to their con-
cept of what was 'right and proper', not to mention 'whole-
some'. If they failed to achieve this, they censured him for not
conforming to their standards. This process has been carried on
well into the present century, and, sad to say, some recent
books still present a distorted picture of the composer.

   The earliest biography of Chopin was written by Liszt, in
French. It has a curious history. The work appeared serially in
1851, and then, slightly expanded, in book form in 1852. The
first English translation, by Martha W Cook, was published in
Philadelphia in 1863. In 1879 another French edition came
out, with substantial additions and changes which seem to have
been largely the work of Liszt's mistress, the Princess Carolyne von
Sayn-Wittgenstein, who had no personal knowledge of Chopin.
This enlarged text was translated by John Broadhouse as *Life
of Chopin* (William Reeves, 1899, last ed 1912). Neither this
nor Martha Cook's version did much justice to the original. But
in 1963, Edward N Waters, the distinguished American Liszt
scholar, produced a new version of Liszt's original French text
(NY, Free Press of Glencoe; Collier-Macmillan), with an important critical and historical introduction. Even when shorn of
the princess's additions, the sense—despite the skilful translation—is often obscure, largely because of the rambling and
high-flown style. The book reads like a sort of romantic commentary, but is significant as the source of some well-known
anecdotes about Chopin, despite the author's limited personal
acquaintance with him.

The first major biography written in English was by Frederick Niecks, *Frederic Chopin as a man and musician* (2 vols, Novello 1888, third ed 1902; pb, NY, Cooper Square 1973), which for many years remained the standard work. Niecks, who became Professor of Music at Edinburgh University, went to immense trouble, and met, or wrote to, all those then living who had known the composer personally. This lends the biographical part of the book a special character, and though later research has revealed its shortcomings, much of what he wrote is of permanent value. But his moralising on Chopin's character and his criticism of the music now seem distinctly outmoded.

This was followed by a smaller work, *Frédéric François Chopin* by Charles Willeby (Sampson Low, 1892), which was virtually a précis of the books by Niecks and Karasowski. For his day, Willeby was unusually censorious about a good deal of Chopin's music. But he could also express appreciation, for instance of the Trio op 8, which was not then very popular. His final verdict was, 'He left the world richer by far than he found it'.

Chopin, by J Cuthbert Hadden, (Dent, 1903, rev ed 1934) was the first biography of him in 'The master musicians' series. Though mostly in the same vein as Willeby, it contains some points of new interest, for instance, a letter (omitted from the 1934 revision) written to the author, at his request by an unknown, and probably not very talented pupil of Chopin. She was a cousin of Jane Stirling, and describes the lessons she had with Chopin in Paris during 1845 and 1846, and the concert he gave in Glasgow in 1848; in spite of a lapse of 57 years, her recollections are remarkably distinct.

An outstanding book was written at the turn of the century by the noted American critic James Huneker, *Chopin, the man and his music* (NY, Scribner. 1900, last ed 1927; William Reeves, 1902). It was greatly in advance of its time for revealing a reasonable and sensible approach to both biography and criticism. It is full of vitality, a quality which is often lacking in other works on Chopin written at this time, and the exuberant

style of writing, though sometimes lacking in considered judgement, is remarkably modern. Huneker's obvious love of the
music and enthusiasm for it is as infectious and alive today as
when he wrote. He had the advantage of having studied to be
a concert pianist. He was sometimes witty at the expense of
fact, but this was rectified in the edition prepared by Herbert
Weinstock (NY, Dover 1966), who added footnotes, corrections and an index and bibliography.

The student of Chopin should not be misled by the title given
by Count Stanislas Tarnowski to his monograph *Chopin: as revealed by extracts from his diary*, translated by Natalie Janotha,
edited by J T Tanqueray (William Reeves, 1906). This is nothing
more than a précis of the early biographies, and has nothing to
do with Chopin's diaries, which (at least in his later years) merely
recorded engagements. The entries Chopin made in a note-
book or album which he had in Vienna and Stuttgart are sometimes referred to as a 'diary' and are always included in editions
of the letters, and these are the main source of the quotations,
which are here coupled with some rather well-worn and sometimes apocryphal anecdotes. Tarnowski also gives a useful syn-
opsis of George Sand's novel *Lucrezia Floriani*, which was based
on her relationship with Chopin in 1846 but has never been
translated into English.

Chopin: the child and the lad, by Zofia Umińska and H E
Kennedy (Methuen, 1925), opens charmingly as might a Victorian children's story. It is indeed intended for children, but
unfortunately there is too much make-believe and not enough
fact. But the many examples of Polish folk-music given throughout are of interest. Guy de Pourtalès' *Frederic Chopin: a man
of solitude*, translated by Charles Bayly (Thornton Butterworth,
1927), had great feeling for the subject and in places is quite
touching, but is, alas, at times both fanciful and inaccurate. The
book mentions two paintings which belonged to Chopin, 'A
caravan in the desert', by Frère, and a pastel of the pyramids,
by Coignet, which, if they could be found, could shed some
light on his artistic tastes. Pourtalès also quotes a remark made
by Chopin to Delacroix: 'You rejoice in your talent with a

sort of security that is a rare privilege and is better than this chase after fame'.

In *Chopin* by Henri Bidou, translated by Catherine Alison Phillips (NY, Alfred Knopf, 1927; Tudor 1936), biography is interspersed with musical analysis in every chapter, which produces a rather chaotic effect. A great deal of space is devoted to paraphrasing George Sand's writings which, though interesting, are undeniably biased. Even so, one can learn things that would otherwise be missed; for example, details of Chopin's and George Sand's stay in Marseilles on their return journey from Majorca in 1839. Bidou, while giving the latter's version of the later rupture between them, points out that she alone spoke and Chopin was silent. Bidou also cites some very curious opinions of Chopin's music expressed by Vincent d'Indy, in particular of the B minor Sonata op 58 which he describes as 'a regular student's exercise, all logic is jealously banished from it'. It is difficult here and there not to be irritated by this book, and yet it is instructive because it gives the point of view of a French writer on Chopin.

Chopin and George Sand in the Cartuja by Ferra Bartomeu (Palma, 1932) is a monograph describing the ill-fated visit to Majorca. The foreword is an extract from the 'Recollections of Aurore Sand', 'Maurice's daughter and George Sand's grand-daughter, who often heard about the visit from them. It also includes a passenger list of *El Mallorquin* showing that George Sand, her children, a maid and Chopin all made the crossing to Majorca from Barcelona on November 7-8, 1838.

Chopin, by Basil Maine (Duckworth, 1933), in the 'Great lives' series, is a short and eminently readable biography. An excellent understanding and knowledge of the composer enabled Maine to paint a sympathetic portrait. He mentions the great beauty of the Barcarolle but points out that it was written in a most discordant atmosphere at Nohant and that Ravel thought the work suggests a 'mysterious apotheosis'.

William Murdoch's *Chopin: his life* (John Murray, 1934; repr Westport, Greenwood, 1971) is by far the best of all the Chopin biographies in English. Although much research has been done since it was written, it still presents a more sensitive and penetrating study of Chopin than can be found elsewhere. Murdoch's balanced understanding of him as a person is free from all Victorian dross and sentimentality, so that a real and life-like character emerges. Writing with the insight of a pianist and musician, Murdoch commands a pleasantly readable style. He treats his subject with dignity and without condescension. The book contains no extensive criticism of the music; Murdoch intended to deal with this in a second volume, but unfortunately died before he could accomplish it.

In 1937 Susanna Brookshaw published privately her monograph *Concerning Chopin in Manchester* (revised edition 1951). It gives many little-known details of his visit in 1848, with pictures of the places he went to and the people he met. There is also a reproduction and a description of Chopin's death mask (now preserved in the Henry Watson Music Library, Manchester), made by the sculptor J B A Clésinger, whom the composer called a 'stone tailor'. The monograph includes a perceptive account of Chopin's playing at the concert that he gave in Manchester: 'We have never heard any public performance so remote from anything like exhibition or display . . . He accomplishes enormous difficulties, but so quietly, so smoothly and with such constant delicacy and refinement that the listener is not sensitive of their real magnitude. It is the exquisite delicacy, with the liquid mellowness of his tone and pearly roundness of his passages of rapid articulation which are the peculiar features of his execution.' One of the other critics at this same concert wrote that he preferred Leopold de Meyer's 'astonishing power, the vigour of Thalberg, the dash of Herz'!

Arthur Hedley's *Chopin* (Dent, 1947) was revised by the author in 1963 and again, after his death, by Maurice Brown in 1973. (It was written to replace the book by Cuthbert Hadden in 'The master musicians' series). Although now nearly 30 years old, Hedley's work is still one of the most up-to-date books in English. It differs from previous ones in that it is not based on either Niecks's book or Opieński's collection of the letters, but on recent Polish and French sources and the author's own extensive researches. The critical section, however, is more subjective and less satisfactory. Hedley's own revision of 1963 included some important changes in the catalogue of works and the date of Chopin's birth. Maurice Brown's revision on one point was unfortunately diametrically opposite to the author's very decided view of the Potocka letters which at this stage, and even in the event of Hedley's view being incorrect, should have been allowed to stand.

Although Herbert Weinstock used the same title as James Huneker's eulogistic book, one is forced to conclude that he often did not share the same sentiments. 'The flower—and cosmetic atmosphere of private salons' is curiously censorious for 1949. He sometimes gives the impression of seeming not to care much about Chopin. His book, *Chopin: the man and his music* (NY, Knopf, 1949) is a sizeable work, almost equally divided between biography and analysis. While the former is perceptive and informative, the critical opinions seem strangely out-of-date. The kind of criticism that could have come from Niecks's pen in 1888 abounds, and indeed Weinstock quotes *verbatim* one of the latter's sillier analyses—that of the Nocturne in G op 37 no 2. Weinstock has attempted to give a phonetic transcription of Polish names, which was a laudable undertaking (even if it does not altogether meet with the approval of some Poles).

Much of *The life and death of Chopin* by Casimir Wierzyński, translated by Norbert Guterman, with a foreword by Artur Rubinstein (Cassell, 1951), is either imaginative or based on memories of the author's childhood. It is sensitively written but tinged and embroidered with his poetic ideas so that it cannot be taken at its face value. He accepts the Potocka letters and quotes from them, but fails to mention, until the end, that they are doubtful. This is a pity, and spoils an otherwise entertaining narrative.

Krystyna Kobylańska's *Chopin in his own land. Documents and souvenirs* (Cracow, Polish Music Publications, 1955), translated by Claire Grece-Dabrowska and Mary Filippi, is an evocative and illuminating book of pictures. It comprises extremely fine reproductions of documents, painting, prints, manuscripts, music—in fact of anything and everything that could be associated with Chopin in Poland up to the time he left there in 1830. For instance, Jan Matuszyński, a boyhood friend of the composer, who was hitherto only a name, suddenly springs to life when one sees his portrait. Here is also a remarkable photographic record of many precious objects which were lost or destroyed in the last war.

Chopin by Camille Bourniquel translated by Sinclair Road (New York, Grove Press, 1960) is a clever book setting out to present a different approach. It has good pictures and is full of the usual anecdotes, many given with a different emphasis or twist, and some of which are new. Yet its facts are by no means correct, and chronology is entirely disregarded. There is no concern for complete accuracy, but much for new presentation. The book is often intriguing, yet frequently irresponsible. For example, to ask anyone to believe that Chopin had a congenital weakness in his fourth fingers is stretching credulity to the point of sheer nonsense.

Chopin: a pictorial biography by André Boucourechliev, translated by Edward Hyams (Thames & Hudson, 1963) is one of the best picture books available in English. Its French counterpart, Robert Bory's *La vie de Frédéric Chopin par l'image*, a better book, has not yet been translated. In points of detail Boucourechliev's text is not always correct, but the pictures are excellent, and the book is well produced. Helpful notes are given about the illustrations and their sources.

Chopin by Joan Chissell (Faber, 1965), is published in "The great composers' series, which is intended for young readers. It offers a lively narrative and contains some excellent photographs, particularly of Majorca. It is clear that the author's vivid descriptions of this island and of Nohant are the result of first-hand experience. Excerpts from a number of Chopin's works are included in the text to encourage further exploration.

Two books of value to the Chopin student, though neither is principally about the composer, are George Sand's *Winter in Majorca*, translated and annotated by Robert Graves (Cassell,

71

1956), and *Jane Wilhelmina Stirling*, by Audrey Evelyn Bone (published privately, 1960). Sand's book gives a vivid picture of the scenery, inhabitants and history of the island where she and the composer spent their traumatic holiday. Graves adds a valuable 'historical summary' which puts the matter in a different perspective. The account of Jane Stirling and her family includes details of Chopin's visit to Scotland which cannot be found elsewhere.

CONTEMPORARY CRITICISM

It was greatly to Schumann's credit that he recognised Chopin's genius as early as 1830, when he praised the op 2 Variations. Schumann's book *On music and musicians* (Dobson, 1947) is culled from criticism written throughout his life, and includes some lively remarks about a dozen or so of Chopin's works. His literary style was inclined to be flowery, in the romantic vein of his age, but his best comments are very much alive and to the point: 'If the Czar knew what a dangerous enemy threatened him in the simple melodies of the mazurkas, he would forbid his music. Chopin's works are guns buried in flowers.' About the consecutive fifths in the Mazurka op 30 no 4 Schumann remarks that the musical pedagogue might learn much from Chopin, above all how to write such a sequence of intervals. He reminds us that once they were perfectly acceptable.

The earliest essay in English on Chopin's music appeared during his lifetime entitled *Essay on the works of Frédéric Chopin* by J W Davison (Wessel, 1843, reprinted by William Reeves, 1935). It was commissioned by Chopin's English publisher Christian Rudolph Wessel to offset the violent attack made in *The musical world* of October 28 1841 (probably by George Macfarren), on the publication of the Four Mazurkas op 41. The essay makes the most extraordinary reading in a highly coloured romantic prose. Davison bestows tremendously fulsome praise on the Nocturnes, Concertos and Studies, and then gives a truly horrific description of the Sonata op 35,

72

after which a hearing of the work would seem like listening to a nursery rhyme.

The famous pianist and conductor Sir Charles Hallé knew Chopin quite well, from 1836 to 1848. His autobiography, edited by Michael Kennedy (Elek, 1972), contains scattered reminiscences, some ten pages in all, which have the ring of rare authenticity. The student will find many other references to Chopin in the writings of Henry F Chorley, critic of *The Athenaeum*, 1830 to 1872. His style is not exactly easy to read but is worth the trouble, for he met Chopin in Paris in 1847 and again when he came to England in 1848. The three books by Chorley containing these references are: *Thirty years' musical recollections* (Hurst & Blackett, 1862; NY, Knopf, 1926), *Music and manners in France and Germany* (Longmans, 1841), *Autobiography, memoir and letters* (Richard Bentley, 1873).

LATER CRITICISM

Sir Henry Hadow's essay in his *Studies in modern music* (Seeley, 1895; Washington, Kennikat Press 1970) starts with a sensitive approach and understanding of the composer, but unfortunately it deteriorates. There is so much adverse academic criticism of the music as to make the second half of little value.

Two books by the Polish critic Jan Kleczyński exemplify the adage that there are few books so bad that they do not contain something of value. They are: *How to play the works of Frédéric Chopin*, translated by Alfred Whittingham (William Reeves, 1880), republished as *Frederick Chopin: an interpretation of his works*, translated by W Kirkbride (Palma de Mallorca, 1970), and *Chopin's greater works* translated by Natalie Janotha (William Reeves, 1912). The ideas on performance put forward in both books are now unacceptable, but the former includes Chopin's own teaching principles and exercises that he sketched out for the 'Méthode des méthodes', and the latter prints some of his directions to his pupils. The 1970 edition of the former book includes 'Chopin's pianos' by Luis Ripoll, translated by

Alan Sillitoe, which should be used with caution as it is regrettably incorrect in technical and historical facts.

A handbook to Chopin's works, by Ashton Jonson (Heinemann, 1905), was written for the advent of the pianola. For a student, it is of historical value as it describes every piece then known and collects writers' opinions about the music. Ignaz Paderewski's *Chopin. A discourse*, translated by Alma-Tadema (William Adlington, 1911), is a prose poem delivered at the Chopin Centenary Festival in Lemberg, October 23, 1910. The great statesman intended to stir the spirit of his country by identifying its aspirations with the emotions aroused by Chopin's music. Paderewski withheld publication in England for about a year because he felt it would not be understood, and it must be admitted that his meaning is sometimes obscure.

ANALYTICAL BOOKS

Three oldish books are still of some value. *Chopin the composer*, by Edgar Stillman Kelley (NY, Schirmer, 1913), is instructive from the technical point of view. Kelley was in advance of his time. He realised how keenly sensitive Chopin was to form, and said that it was as absurd to criticise him for not writing sonatas in the style of Beethoven as it would be to belittle the latter for not composing fugues after the manner of Bach. Kelley's remarks on the orchestra of 1830 are revealing and deserve study.

Most of *Chopin's ornamentation*, by John Petrie Dunn (Novello, 1921) states the obvious in many respects, and the remarks about *rubato* are decidedly suspect. It does however offer some useful definitions in the section preceding Part I. Mania Seguel's *Chopin's tempo rubato* (Altham, nr Accrington, Old Parsonage Press, 1928) gives only part of the truth about this complex topic, which is so frequently misunderstood. It should be remembered that true *rubato* cannot be taught; it is the teaching of an approximation which is so dangerous.

How Chopin played by Edith J Hipkins (Dent, 1937), contains contemporary impressions, collected from the diaries and notebooks of her father, A J Hipkins (1826-1903), who met Chopin and heard him play many times at Broadwood's in 1848, and also tuned pianos for him. On one point Hipkins's notes were incorrect, for when describing the visual effect of Chopin's playing, he wrote that he kept his elbows close to his sides, and played only with finger touch, using no weight from the arm. This is how it may have appeared to Hipkins. But Chopin himself wrote that 'to attempt to play entirely from the wrist, as Kalkbrenner advocates, is incorrect'. Obviously Chopin would not have done so. It is often impossible to see when the weight of the arm is being utilised. Unfortunately Edith Hipkins saw fit to intrude her own ideas, without verifying them, and some are far from correct. This seems to have led some writers to disparage Hipkins and reject the book, which is a pity. The essence of the chapter 'The art of the early piano' is good, but it is not true to say that 'to find the real Chopin we want the early square piano'. We need in fact the wooden-framed grand piano, made between 1830 and 1850, a very different matter. Again, in connection with Chopin's early Mazurkas, the term 'Bebung' ('vibrato'), as employed on a clavichord, is mentioned, but it is confused with *rubato*.

Chopin's musical style (OUP, 1939, pb) by Gerald Abraham has become the standard book. It traces the growth of Chopin's musical style from 1822 onwards, and divides its development into three periods: I Evolution of a musical personality (1822-1831); II Chopin's mature style (1831-1840); III The last phase (1841-1849). It is possible to argue that three divisions are somewhat arbitrary, and that a single division, at 1841, as noted by Cortot, is preferable. Masterly as is the author's grasp of technical analysis, one cannot help feeling that he sometimes suggests that Chopin approached harmony in a rather academic and intellectual way, whereas many of his most remarkable achievements seem rather to have been the result of pure intuition. For the historically-minded reader this is a fascinating and indispensable book. It shows how Chopin's genius matured

75

and how his unique gifts put him on a different plane from his lesser contemporaries. It also reveals the unexpected extent to which earlier musicians influenced him (Abraham's underestimation of J S Bach is surprising), and even more interestingly, the composers whom he influenced both during his life and long after his death.

The main interest in Alfred Cortot's book *In search of Chopin*, translated by Cyril and Rena Clarke (Peter Nevill, 1951), lies in the fact that its author was a famous interpreter of Chopin. As a whole, it is a curious mixture, both as to subject matter and quality. The most valuable chapter is that entitled 'Chopin the pedagogue' which contains *exactly* what he left of the sketch for his 'Méthode des méthodes'. The title of the final chapter, 'He was not like other men', comes from Jane Stirling, and is—to say the least—misleading. In general, Cortot relied too much on second-hand information, even, unfortunately, on fiction, and the book abounds in mistakes, both of spelling and fact.

A symposium, by eleven writers, entitled *Chopin: profiles of the man and the musician*, edited by Alan Walker (Barrie & Rockliff, 1966), is of unequal merit. Arthur Hutchings writes instructively on 'The historical background'; Peter Gould discusses the Sonatas and Concertos with much insight. Humphrey Searle brings knowledge and sympathy to 'Miscellaneous works'—for piano and orchestra, chamber music and piano solo —drawing attention to some that are unduly neglected. Two outstanding chapters are by Alan Rawsthorne, who deals with the Ballades, the Fantasy in F minor and the Scherzi in an excellent, unpedantic style, and by Sir Lennox Berkeley, who, like Rawsthorne, writes with the understanding of a composer. Sir Lennox discusses with great insight and the minimum of technical jargon Chopin's genius as found in the Nocturnes, Berceuse and Barcarolle. There is much originality in Bernard Jacobson's essay on the songs, which could be profitably studied by singers. The essential English translations are well done. There is a fairly comprehensive discography.

MISCELLANEOUS

Adam Harasowski's *The skein of legends about Chopin* (Glasgow, William Maclellan, 1967) is of very mixed value. It includes the summary, already mentioned, of the controversy about the Potocka letters. The bulk of the work comprises critiques of 42 books on Chopin, by a great variety of writers, and of varying merit. In trying to show how their authors have contributed to the legends about the composer, Harasowski is, for the most part, negative beyond endurance. It is, however, useful to have substantial extracts from books by Polish authors, such as Hoesick, not otherwise translated into English. We learn, incidentally, that *The shape of love* by Broszkiewicz (1955) tries to show that Chopin was a communist!

The Chopin Society in Warsaw has issued *Studies in Chopin* (1973), edited by Dariusz Zebrowski, translated by Eugenie Taska, Halina Oszczygiel and Luwik Wiewiórkowski. It comprises seven scholarly essays, including 'The musical reception of Chopin's works' (Zofia Lissa), 'Chopin and his contemporaries, Paris 1832-1860' (Olgierd Pisarenko), 'Studies of the Chopin melodic design' (Zofia Chechlińska). The last two, 'Registers of Chopin manuscripts in Polish collections' (Teresa Dalila Turlo), and 'Chopin's biography: contemporary research and history' (Krystyna Kobylańska), are especially valuable to the student. The latter, in particular, sheds considerable light on the immense pitfalls and difficulties there are in reaching the truth of the 'facts' of Chopin's life. Krystyna Kobylańska also classifies the different types of biography that exist, for instance: vie romancée, biographical story, research works; and she points out how one type, particularly the vie romancée, takes over information from another.

John Field and Chopin by David Branson (Barrie & Jenkins, 1972) is a study of the influence of Field on Chopin. It is at times illuminating and revealing, even if the case for Field's originality is somewhat overstated. But it is questionable whether it is really worthwhile to draw so much attention

77

to a very faint and possibly fortuitous likeness between a number of passages in works by these two composers.

The most recent book on the composer is by Ates Orga (Midas Books, 1976); *Chopin: his life and times* is a short biography well illustrated and attractively produced. Though perceptive and often poetic, it is somewhat uneven. Long stretches of time are compressed into a few sentences which is a pity. The best part of the book is about George Sand's *Lucrezia Floriani*, and points out the similarities between this work and her autobiography. The account of Solange's marriage and the break up between George Sand and Chopin is also well done. There are some excellent pictures, though one of Chopin is given as being of Liszt, but there is an erratum slip in the first edition.

Editions of Chopin's music

By November 1847 Chopin had published all the compositions that he intended the public to have up to that time. During the remaining two years of his life he wrote only one song, Melodya, a Waltz (in B major) which is unpublished, and two Mazurkas in G minor and F minor which were published posthumously as op 67 no 2 and op 68 no 4 respectively.

At the time of Chopin's death, his portfolio contained about forty compositions of varying lengths, among them the Fantasie-Impromptu and the Rondo for two pianos. He asked that all of them should be destroyed, but this was not done. Many of the pieces were juvenilia, but this group also includes sixteen songs which were written at different times throughout his life.

The first of the posthumous publications were the Variations on a German air 'The Swiss Boy', and the Sonata op 4. These were brought out by Haslinger in 1851; the Sonata had been sent to him by Elsner in 1828 and Chopin had left the Variations with the publisher when he first went to Vienna in 1829.

The main collection of the posthumous works was published by Chopin's friend Julian Fontana in 1855 and comprised op 66 to 73. Sixteen of the songs were published two years later as op 74. During roughly the next century thirty-two small works have come to light, comprising the seventy-three pieces which complete the total of all Chopin's posthumous works that have so far been found.

79

THEMATIC CATALOGUES

The first thematic catalogue was compiled by one of Chopin's publishers, Breitkopf & Härtel, in 1852, three years after his death. It was revised in 1888. It held the field for over a century but has been entirely superseded by *Chopin: an index of his works in chronological order* by Maurice J E Brown (Macmillan, London and New York, 1960, revised second edition 1972). This is a wholly admirable book and is essential for any serious study of Chopin. It is of inestimable value in placing or dating a work, which is often essential for understanding and appreciation. Besides giving the chronological order of the complete works, the catalogue sets out full particulars of each composition—publication, dedication, the whereabouts of the manuscripts and their dates. There are also nine appendices and four indices:

Appendices
   I   Chronological sequence of publication
  II   Publishers of the first editions
 III   Complete editions
 IV   Wessel's complete edition
  V   Dedications
 VI   The poets of Chopin's songs
VII   Chopin's addresses in Paris
VIII   Three autograph albums
 IX   Bibliography
Indices
1 Works arranged in catalogues
2 Works with opus numbers
3 Works without opus numbers
4 General index

Chopin's publishers

Chopin's first two publishers were J J Cybulski, an Abbé and proprietor of a small music printing business near St Mary's Church in Warsaw, who published the seven-year-old composer's Polonaise in G minor in 1817, and Andrea Brzezina & Co,

Warsaw, who published his Rondo op 1 in 1825. His last publishers were three: Breitkopf & Härtel in Leipzig, Brandus in Paris, and Wessel in London, who brought out the three Waltzes op 64 in 1847-48, which were the final works to be published in the composer's lifetime. The last edition was Wessel's which came out in September 1848, while Chopin was in Scotland.

In the thirty years between 1817 and 1847 Chopin himself had dealings with twenty-one publishers, chief among whom were Wessel & Co in England, Schlesinger in France and Breitkopf & Härtel in Germany. Since his death his music has grown in popularity to the extent of being published all over the world in a vast and ever-increasing number of editions. Some of them, issued towards the end of the last century and in the first quarter of the present, have been over-edited. For example, it is not uncommon to find additional dynamic markings and a superfluity of extra phrase and expression marks. Some works are smothered in entirely unnecessary and often unsuitable fingering. Ganche pointed out in the preface to his edition that 'a reviser would be no reviser if he did not revise!'.

The first editions are models of what they should be and show exactly what the composer intended. They are clear, uncluttered with unnecessary dynamic and phrase markings, and well spaced so that the text is, above all, easy to read.

THE COMPLETE EDITIONS

Maurice Brown lists nine complete editions which were selected only from those 'with some claim to having been based on original material'. They are as follows, in chronological order:

1 The earliest was Wessel & Co's (London c1853), who produced the most complete edition before that of Breitkopf & Härtel (no 5 below) and which comprised 71 items and is now very scarce.

2 In 1860 Simon Richault, Paris, brought out a 'new and cheap Paris edition'. This was edited in 12 volumes by a Norwegian pupil of Chopin's, Thomas Tellefsen (who, rather

curiously, taught Jane Stirling in Norway, after Chopin's death. She had previously been a pupil of the composer's for six or seven years). It excluded the songs. Tellefsen studied only for a short time with Chopin.

3 The composer's family authorised the third complete edition which was published in 1863 by Gebethner of Warsaw. Like the previous two editions it omitted the songs.

4 Karl Klindworth, a pupil of Liszt, was responsbile for an edition which contained the piano works only, and which was published by P Jurgenson of Moscow, 1873-1876. Klindworth sometimes considered that he knew better than Chopin, for example, in the choice of note-values of the opening of the Polonaise-Fantasie op 61. Later this edition was enlarged to include the works with orchestra and was revised by X Scharwenka. In the UK the edition is often referred to as 'Augener' as it is published by this firm. It is an edition which has been over-edited and is visually unpleasing.

5 Breitkopf & Härtel's edition was issued in 1878-1880. They had the advantage of having been one of the original publishers of Chopin, and their first editions are, of course, of great importance. They used these and the original MSS from which to prepare a new complete edition. Unfortunately there were no less than six editors, only one of whom, the 'cellist Franchomme, had any real connection with Chopin. Amongst the others **were** Brahms and Liszt, two musicians very far removed from Chopin in outlook. The order was

1 Ballades	5 Polonaises	9 Waltzes
2 Studies	6 Preludes	10 Various works
3 Mazurkas	7 Rondos & Scherzi	11 Piano and string instruments
4 Nocturnes	8 Sonatas	12 Piano & orchestra

6 Another Leipzig edition, issued by F Kistner, also one of Chopin's original publishers, is exceedingly valuable because the editor, Karl Mikuli, was a pupil of Chopin for four years. As a basis, he used the composer's notes and his set of the French first editions which, because they were often corrected

in proof by Chopin himself, are more significant than the German or English editions. Mikuli states that Chopin, when teaching him, used the French editions and that he corrected misprints whenever he noticed them. One of Mikuli's difficulties was to establish priority. As the original English and German editions often came out later than the French one, they too contain corrections, alterations and improvements made in proof by Chopin himself. (Even after a work was published Chopin was known to alter it, perhaps for a pupil, so that in some cases there may not be one definitive contemporary edition, but as many as three.) Mikuli's edition was reprinted by G Schirmer of New York in 1949. The order of the two editions is as follows:

(a) *Kistner*

1 Mazurkas	7 Sonatas	13 Fantasia, etc
2 Nocturnes	8 Waltzes	14 Various: Barcarolle, Berceuse, etc
3 Studies	9 Rondos	15 Concertos
4 Ballades	10 Scherzi	16 Chamber music
5 Polonaises	11 Impromptus	17 Piano parts (Supplement)
6 Preludes	12 Variations	

(b) *Schirmer*

1 Waltzes	6 Impromptus	11 Sonatas
	7 Scherzi &	12 Miscellaneous
2 Mazurkas	Fantasie	13 Four concert
3 Polonaises	8 Studies	pieces
4 Nocturnes	9 Preludes	14 Concerto I
5 Ballades	10 Rondos	15 Concerto II

7 C F Peters was the third Leipzig publisher to bring out a complete edition, in three volumes in 1879. It was edited by Hermann Scholtz, who used autograph and various printed editions which, again, had been corrected by Chopin for two of his pupils, Mlle R de Könneritz and Georges Mathias. It is not visually a good edition, as it is very cramped.

8 There was then a gap of over fifty years before the eighth and penultimate edition appeared. This might be described as an Anglo-French edition, as it was published by the Oxford University Press, London, in 1932, but edited by Edouard Ganche, President of the Frédéric Chopin Society in Paris. It was in three volumes and comprised the piano works only. Ganche based his work on original French editions which had belonged to Jane Stirling, and were corrected by Chopin himself. Jane Stirling left them to her sister Anne Houston, and they were in turn inherited by the latter's grand-daughter, who made them available to Ganche. It was a complete return to the original editions, and in spite of some doubtful pieces for which uncorrected or unchecked mss were used—for example, the first of the Trois Nouvelles Etudes—it is a very valuable edition. It is now out of print and should be reprinted. The order in the three volumes is:

Vol I	Vol II	Vol III
Preludes	Ballades	Mazurkas
Studies	Impromptus	Morceau de con-
Waltzes	Scherzi &	cert
Nocturnes	Fantasie	Concertos
Polonaises	Rondeaux	Rondo for two
	Berceuse, Barca-	pianos
	rolle	
	Variations and	
	Sonatas	

9 The definitive edition is the *Polish complete edition* (Warsaw 1949-1962) edited by Ignacy Jan Paderewski (1860-1941), Ludwig Broñarski and Josef Turczyński, in twenty-seven volumes, any one of which can be bought singly. This is complete and up-to-date, and provides scholarly commentaries on every piece. It was initiated by the Fryderyk Chopin Institute in Warsaw, and is now the best text available. The editors have taken enormous care and trouble to provide an authentic and final text, as far as it is possible to achieve this with Chopin. All worthwhile variants from other reputable editions are mentioned in the commentaries. The Polish edition is based on

original mss and first editions, and it offers the highest standards of musical scholarship. It is also as clear visually as were the first and early editions. The edition (referred to later as CE) is arranged as follows:

I	Preludes	XI	Fantasia, Berceuse, Barcarolle
II	Studies	XII	Rondos
III	Ballades	XIII	Concert Allegro, Variations
IV	Impromptus	XIV	Concertos
V	Scherzos	XV	Works for piano & orchestra
VI	Sonatas	XVI	Chamber music
VII	Nocturnes	XVII	Songs
VIII	Polonaises	XVIII	Minor works
IX	Waltzes	XIX-XXI	Orchestral scores
X	Mazurkas	XXII-XXVII	Orchestral parts

LARGE COLLECTIONS

Debussy edited the complete piano works, which were published by Durand et fils, Paris, in twelve volumes. The text is visually somewhat cramped and the grouping is rather unsystematic:

1	Waltzes	7	Mazurkas
2	Preludes & Rondos	8	Berceuse, Barcarolle, Variations
3	Ballades & Impromptus	9	Sonatas
4	Studies	10	Scherzi & Fantasie
5	Nocturnes	11	Morceau de concert
6	Polonaises	12	Concertos

The pianist Alfred Cortot produced what he termed a 'working edition'—*Edition de travail des oeuvres de Chopin*, published by Editions Salabert, Paris. The text, for example, of both the Studies and the Preludes includes about two pages of Cortot's advice, instructions and preliminary exercises for every piece. These may be useful, and sometimes invaluable, but are also somewhat daunting! Only three of the thirteen volumes seem to have been translated into English, namely the Studies, Preludes and Ballades. The edition cannot be described as visually pleasing: there are six double staves on every page, often with long footnotes in small print, and music examples for practice in even smaller type wherever there is no detailed preface to each work. Again, the order is chaotic; there is no numbering of the volumes, which are listed in the following order:

Studies op 10	Pièces Diverses	Oeuvres Posthumes:
Studies op 25	Vol I: Fantasie,	Op 4, Op 71, Op 72,
Preludes	Barcarolle, Ber-	A, B, & C
Ballades	ceuse, Taran-	Polonaise Posthume
Sonatas	telle	en Sol dièze mineur
Scherzi	Vol II: Allegro	
Impromptus	de concert,	
Waltzes	Boléro, Trois	
Nocturnes 2 vols	Nouvelles Etudes,	
Mazurkas 3 vols	Prelude op 45	
Polonaises	Variations op 12	

Schirmer (NY), as well as reprinting Mikuli's edition, also brought out one by the Hungarian pianist Rafael Joseffy. Although it appears a fairly good edition and was considered authoritative, it cannot compare with the Polish CE, with Mikuli, or with Ganche. Neither is it complete. The order of the volumes is as follows:

1 Waltzes	7 Scherzi & Fantasy
2 Mazurkas	8 Studies (edited by Friedheim)
3 Not published	9 Preludes
4 Nocturnes	10 Rondos
5 Ballades	11 Concert pieces
6 Impromptus	

There is a *Chopin edition for students* by Frank Merrick (Novello). It is, visually, a very passable edition, clearly printed on good paper. But there are some inaccuracies, for example, a bar which Chopin deleted from the Nocturne op 37 no 2 is

86

described as being an extra bar inserted by Chopin. Chopin's extremely important phrasing marks in the F major Ballade op 38 are omitted. Merrick clumsily corrects Chopin's arithmetically incorrect notation of the first Prelude of op 28. All the pedal and metronome markings are by Merrick, who, however, follows the scholarly practice of putting his own expression marks in brackets. The following eight volumes are available:

Waltzes	Preludes	Mazurkas
Impromptus	Ballades	Scherzos
Nocturnes	Studies	

MISCELLANEOUS EDITIONS

PIANO MUSIC

The following list gives various existing editions, some of them modern, as alternatives to the CE, Mikuli or Ganche. It includes, at the end, the few works not included in the CE or in the earlier editions, and some of those without opus numbers. It is arranged under fourteen different headings and gives the titles of the works in the same order as in the CE, with the exception of the last volume which is no XVIII in the CE. In some cases there are no worthwhile alternatives and only CE is given. The word 'by' is here equivalent to 'edited by'. Where a work has no opus number, Brown's numbering is used. Publishers' names are given in full except for the following:

Brit Con = British and Continental
C = Curwen
H = Henle (Munich)
OUP = Oxford University Press
S = Schott
S/C = Schirmer/Chappell (NY, London)
SCH = Schirmer (NY)
UE = Universal Edition (Vienna & London)

When no town is given the place of publication is London. The place of publication and the editor's initials are omitted when either recurs several times in succession. Publishers' addresses are most readily available in the *British catalogue of music* (issued by the Bibliographical Services Division of the British Library, which is to be found in major public libraries throughout the world). Besides the addresses of all British music publishers, this catalogue includes those of the leading American firms and those of many European firms which have branches in London.

Works for piano solo

1   *Preludes* op 28, 45. (CE I), by Hermann Keller (H). The Henle edition is extremely good and is strongly to be recommended; by Hansen and J Demus (UE); by York Bowen (Brit Con).

2   *Studies* op 10, 25 and the Trois Nouvelles Etudes (Brown 130) (CE II) by E Zimmermann and H Keller (H); by P Badura-Skoda (UE); Study in F minor no 1 from the Trois Nouvelles Etudes, authentic text (with editorial notes by A Hedley) published privately.

3   *Ballades* op 23, 38, 47, 52 (CE III), by York Bowen (Brit Con).

4   *Impromptus* op 29, 36, 51, 66 (CE IV) by Bronislaw von Pozniak (Peters); Fantasie-impromptu op 66 by Artur Rubinstein (Sch).

5   *Scherzi* op 20, 31, 39, 54 (CE V) by E Zimmermann (H); by York Bowen (Brit Con).

6   *Sonatas* op 4, 35, 58 (CE VI); Sonata op 4 by Louis Köhler (Litolff), by A Ikelmer (Paris, Bibliothèque universelle du pianiste); Sonata op 35 in B flat minor and Sonata op 58 in B minor by T Kullak (Sch), by Köhler (Litolff), by R Pugno (UE), by A Brugnoli (Ricordi).

7   *Nocturnes* (CE VII) by E Zimmermann and H M Theopold (H); by R Pugno (UE); by York Bowen (Brit Con). Nocturne in C sharp minor (Brown no 49) by S Niedzielski (Augener), and by Francis L York (Sch). Nocturne in C minor (Brown no 108) by Jack Werner (Elkin).

8   *Polonaises* (CE VIII); Polonaise in A flat op 53 (Ashdown, successors to Wessel).

9   *Waltzes* (CE IX) by E Zimmermann and H M Theopold
(H) (this is the most complete edition to date); by York Bowen
(Brit Con) and by Raoul Pugno (UE) which include Waltzes only
up to no 14 in E minor op posth, which was first published in
1868; Waltz in E flat (Brown no 133) first published in 1955
with postscript by Maurice Brown (Francis, Day and Hunter);
Waltz in A minor (Brown no 150) by Jack Werner (Curwen)
1958.

10   *Mazurkas* (CE X) by E Zimmermann and H M Theopold
(H); by R Pugno (UE); last Mazurka op 68 no 4 in F minor by
Ronald Smith (Shattinger-International Music Corporation NY
and Hansen House, London, 1975)—it includes an Episode in
F major which Fontana and Franchomme omitted when it was
first published in 1855 and which is not in the CE either; and
by Jan Ekier (Kraków) in 1965. A Mazurka and a Contre-danse
(Brown no 17) by Jack Werner (Curwen) (Sch) in 1958.

11   Fantasia op 49, Berceuse op 57, Barcarolle op 60 (CE
XI).

12   *Rondos* op 1, 5, 16, and op 73 for solo and for two
pianos (CE XII); op 73 for two pianos by E Hughes (Sch) 1927
(Reissued, London, printed 1950).

13   Concert Allegro op 46 and *Variations* (CE XIII); (in
this volume of the CE the variations consist of the following:
on a German Air, sometimes called 'The Swiss boy (Brown no
14); Souvenir de Paganini (Brown no 37) and the E major for the
Hexameron Variations (Brown no 113); Souvenir de Paganini
(Brown no 37) by Jack Werner (Elkin).

14   *Minor works* Boléro op 19, Tarantelle op 43 and eleven
posthumous works (CE XVIII), which consist of two editions
of a funeral march op 72 no 2, Trois Ecossaises op 72 nos 3, 4
& 5, Nocturne in C minor (Brown no 108), Nocturne in C sharp
minor (Brown no 49), Contre-danse (Brown no 17), Cantabile
(Brown no 84), Album leaf or Moderato (Brown no 151), Largo
(Brown no 109) and Fugue (Brown no 144). There are Variations in D major for piano duet listed in the second edition of
his *Index* (12A) (not in CE), by Jan Ekier (Polskie Wydawnictwo Muzycne, Cracow 1965).

The Tarantelle op 43 was first published by Schuberth (Hamburg and Leipzig) in 1841 in an edition for four hands as well as for piano solo. This is not mentioned by Brown. It is the only instance in the British Library Music Catalogue of a piano solo work by Chopin having been published for four hands at the same time as the first solo edition. This may account for Chopin's negotiating with Breitkopf & Härtel for publishing the work a month after Schuberth had paid him for it. It is curious that a work Chopin himself was inclined to deprecate should have been published in two forms.

Other works, not in the CE, are Three Piano Pieces, by Ates Orga (Schott, 1968). They are a piano arrangement, made by Chopin, of the song 'Wiosna' ('Spring') (Brown no 117), and Two Bourrées (Brown no 160B).

Piano concertos op 11, 21 (CE XIV) by A Ruthardt (Peters) —unlike many editions of the concertos, this has the orchestral part arranged for a second piano and printed below the solo part; both concertos with foreword by S Askenase (Eulenburg pocket scores).

Works for piano and orchestra op 2, 13, 14, 22 (CE XV); Fantasie on Polish Airs op 13, part of the 'complete works revised by C Klindworth and X Scharwenka' (with the orchestral tuttis reduced to piano parts) (Augener) 1934 sold separately; Krakowiak op 14 by C Mikuli (Kistner), second piano replaces orchestral accompaniment.

CHAMBER MUSIC

Op 3, 8, 65, Grand Duo and Variations for flute (CE XXI).

Variations on a theme by Rossini by Jean-Pierre Rampal (International Music Co, NY, 1960).

Introduction and polonaise op 3 by M Gendron and J Français (Schott).

Trio for pfte, vln, 'cello op 8 by F David (Kistner).

Sonata for 'cello op 65 by L Schulz (Sch); also by M Balakirev, and *Polonaise* op 3 by F Grützmacher, (Peters); Sonata op 65 by L Grützmacher (Litolff); arranged for violin by F David (Breitkopf & Härtel).

VOCAL WORKS

Nineteen Polish Songs (CE XVII)—seventeen songs with
English words 'Translated through the German of F Gumbert'
by the Rev J Troutbeck, (Stanley Lucas, Weber & Co); also
Seventeen Polish Songs in the original keys with English and
Polish words, English version by J Sliwinski (Paterson's Publi-
cations, 1941). As a curiosity, and because Chopin often heard
Pauline Viardot sing, some of his Mazurkas, the following is in-
cluded: op 6 no 1, Plainte d'Amour, arr par Mme P Viardot
(Gebethner & Wolf, Warsaw) c1900.

FACSIMILES are used as frontispieces to nearly all the volumes
of the Polish CE, some having as many as three. There are also
some in Ganche's edition (OUP). A facsimile of an original ms,
of perhaps an over-familiar work, can make a surprising impact
and give a freshness of outlook to a performer. Chopin's cal-
ligraphy is minute and often exquisite.

Facsimiles of the following works have been published in
Poland as a numbered series (all by Wladislaw Hordynski):

op 28 Twenty-four Preludes
op 47 Ballade in A flat
op 38 Ballade in F major
op 60 Barcarolle
op 14 Krakowiak
op 58 Sonata in B minor
op 54 Scherzo in E major
op 31 Scherzo in B flat minor
op 2 Variations on 'Là ci darem' by Mozart
op 49 Fantasia

Variations for four hands in D major (Polskie Wydawnictwo
Muzycne, Cracow 1951-66).

Ballade op 38, Waltz op 69 no 1, Berceuse op 57, commentary by Alfred Cortot, history of mss by E Ganche (in French),
Paris 1932.

Tarantelle op 43, (Paul Catin, Paris, 1930).

Etude op 10 no 3, (Robert Owen Lehman Foundation, Washington, 1964).

Selected recordings of Chopin's music

Ideally, only recordings which approximate to the spirit of the composer and his style of playing should be considered, but on this basis only a very few records of complete works or of isolated movements would qualify for inclusion. In any case, for certain works the current range of choice is surprisingly limited. The order of presentation of records of any one work does not indicate personal preference or degree of excellence. Where there is a strong personal recommendation, the entry is marked by an asterisk.

It should be remembered that some well-known interpreters of Chopin are distinctly uneven. Because one work appeals to a pianist and may be superbly interpreted by him, it does not necessarily mean that he will attain that same standard in all the other works he essays.

When a recording in the list has been deleted, it may be possible to borrow it from one of the many public gramophone libraries in both the United Kingdom and the United States. Quite often a full-price recording reappears on a cheaper label after its deletion at the higher price.

Any second catalogue number given is American. If there is no second number, the recordings may not be available in America except by import. Sometimes a different selection of secondary items played by the same artist can be found under an identical main subject; these have not been included. American readers are referred to the excellent *Schwann* catalogue for a complete listing of American recordings, which include many only available in the United States.

For records that were available in 1951, the reader is referred to the discography compiled by Cyril Clarke in Alfred Cortot's *In search of Chopin* (see page 76); and the discography compiled by Alan Walker in his symposium *Frédéric Chopin: profiles of the man and the musician* (see page 76) gives records that were available in 1966.

Record enthusiasts who are interested in the historical aspect of the interpretation of Chopin's music may find it worthwhile searching for records cut during the first three decades of this century by one of the earliest of Chopin's interpreters, Vladimir de Pachmann (1848-1933). Some discs have been re-recorded.

Discounting records that have been made from piano-rolls, for these cannot be entirely trusted, extraordinarily brilliant performances do exist on records of pianists like Moritz Rosenthal (who was a pupil of Mikuli), and Josef Lhevinne. These early records can show how some aspects of piano-playing have improved; for instance, general musicianship and adherence to the text. But some of them make us realise how less desirable changes have occurred. In place of a consistently beautiful touch we now have, all too often, one of relentless machine-like precision which ruins the enjoyment of the music.

This list has been divided into four sections, following the plan of the current *Gramophone classical catalogue*.

WORKS WITH ORCHESTRA (op 2, 11, 13, 14, 21, 22)

Andante Spianato and Grand Polonaise in E flat op 22
    Rubinstein; New York Sym of Air; Wallenstein. DPS 2034; 2RCA LSC 2265.
    Weissenberg; Paris Conservatoire; Skrowaczewski. ASD 2371.
Piano Concerto no 1 in E minor op 11
    *Lipatti; orchestra unknown, recording of a concert in May 1948. HQM 1248; SERA 60007. With Nocturne in D flat, op

27 no 2; Mazurka in C sharp minor, op 50 no 3; Waltz in A flat, op 34 no 1. (These three pieces were recorded in a studio and the playing is not to be compared with the spontaneous performance of the concerto.)

Ohlsson; Polish Radio Sym; Maksymiuk. SLS 5043.

Pollini; Phi; Kletzki. SXLP 30160; SERA S-60066.

Rubinstein; New Sym; Skrowaczewski. DPS 2034; London RCA LSC-2575.

Piano Concerto no 2 in F minor op 21

Rubinstein; New York Sym of Air; Wallenstein. DPS 2034; RCA LSC-2265 Larrocha; Suisse; Comissiona. SXL 6258.

Larrocha; Suisse; Comissiona. SXL 6258. With Falla's Nights in the Gardens of Spain.

V Ashkenazy; LSO; Zinman. SXL 6174; London 6440. With Bach Harpsicord Concerto no 1.

*Haskil; Lamoureux; Markevitch. ABL 3340; stereo SABL 173 (835 072 AY). With Falla's Nights in the Gardens of Spain.

Ohlsson; Polish Radio Sym; Maksymiuk. SLS 5043.

Fantasy on Polish Airs op 13

Weissenberg; Paris Conservatoire; Skrowaczewski. ASD 2371; 3ANG S-3723.

Kedra; National Phil Sym Warsaw; Rowicki. XL 0076.

Krakowiak op 14

Weissenberg; Paris Conservatoire; Skrowaczewski; ASD 2371; 3ANG S-3723.

Kedra; Nat Phil Sym Warsaw; Rowicki. XL 0076.

S Askenase; Hague PO; Otterloo. 2548 066. With Piano Concerto no 1.

Variations 'La cî darem la mano' (Mozart) op 2

Weissenberg; Paris Conservatoire; Skrowaczewski. ASD 2371; 3 ANG S-3723.

Kedra; Nat Phil Sym Warsaw; Rowicki. XL 0076.

CHAMBER WORKS (op 3, 8, 65 and two works without op nos)

Grand Duo on themes from 'Robert le Diable' (Meyerbeer)
Navarra, J-M Darré. SAGA 5166 (there is a cut made).

Halina Kowalska (cello); Wladyslaw Szpilman (piano); XL 0080.

Introduction and Polonaise op 3
Halina Kowalska, Wladystaw Szpilman; XL 0080.
Navarra, J-M Darré. SAGA 5166 (the text has been altered).
Rostropovich (Monitor S-2119E, American only).

Piano Trio in G minor op 8
Beaux Arts Trio. With Smetana Piano Trio. 6500 133. Phil 6500 133.
*Wladyslaw Szpilman, Tadeusz Wronski, Aleksander Ciechanski; XL 0081.

Sonata for cello and piano in G minor op 65
Du Pré, Barenboim. With Franck Cello Sonata. ASD 2851; ANG S-36937.
Kazimierz Witkomirski (cello), Maria Witkomirska (piano); XL 0081.
Tortelier, Ciccolini. With Rachmaninov Cello Sonata. ASD 2587.

Variations for flute and piano on a theme from Rossini's Cenerentola
Wlodzimierz Tomaszczuk (flute), Barbara Hesse-Bukowska (piano); XL 0079.

PIANO SOLO

Allegro de concert op 46
Barbara Hesse-Bukowska; XL 0079.
Arrau. With Studies. (American only; ANG 35413.)

Ballades op 23, 38, 47, 52
1-4 Rubinstein. SB 2082; RCA LSC-2370.
1-4 V Ashkenazy. With Trois Nouvelles Etudes; SXL 6143; LON 6422.
No 3 Pachmann. Recital GEM 103.

Barcarolle op 60
*Lipatti. HQM 1163.
Rubinstein. Recital SB 6683.
V Ashkenazy. With Scherzi. SXL 6334. With Piano Concerto no 2 in F minor, SXL 6693.

Berceuse op 57
  Solomon. RLS 701.
  Larrocha. SXL 6733.
  Rubinstein. SB 6683.
Bolero op 19
  Rubinstein. SB 6683.
  R Smith. HQS 1290.
Three Écossaises op 72
  R Smith. HQS 1290.
  Milkina. TPLS 13050-1. (Two recitals, but with only one other Chopin work included; four sides, not available separately.)
Etudes op 10, nos 1-12, op 25, nos 13-24
  1-24, Pollini. 2530 291; DG 2530291.
  1-24, V Ashkenazy. SXL 6710; LON 6844.
  1-24, Novaes. 510 930; VOX 510930E.
Trois Nouvelles Etudes (nos 25-27)
  V Ashkenazy. With the four Ballades. SXL 6143. LON 6422.
  Rubinstein. Recital, SB 6683.
Fantasia in F minor op 49
  Rubinstein. Recital SB 6683.
  Ohlsson. HQS 1328. ANG S-37017.
  Solomon. Recital (six sides not available separately) RLS 701.
Fantasie Impromptu op 66
  Magaloff. ECS 513.
  Rubinstein. SER 6874.
  Moiseiwitsch. SXLP 30075.
  S Askenase. 2538 078.
Impromptus op 29, 36, 51
  Rubinstein. SB 6649. 2 RCA LSC 7037.
  Magaloff ECS 513.
  S Askenase. 2538 078.
Mazurkas (complete 1-58)
  Magaloff. ECS 620-1; 3 Lon STS 1514 6/8.
  Milkina (Six sides not available separately.) TPLS 13038.

R Smith. (Six sides not available separately.) SLS 5014.
Rubinstein. Nos 1-51 SB 6702-4; 3RCA LSC 6177.
Nocturnes (21) complete
Weissenberg. Nos 1-21 SLS 838; 2A NG S-3747.
Rubinstein. 1-19 SB 6731-2; 2RCA LSC 7050.
Polonaises (16)
Frankl 1-16 (four sides) TV 34254-5S.
Czerny-Stefanska, Jan Ekier, L Stefanski 1-16; with Andante
Spianato. (Six sides not available separately.) ERA 9055-7.
Ohlsson 1-16 and Andante Spianato SLS 843; 2ANG S 3794.
Preludes op 28, 45, in A flat (Brown 8b)
Eschenbach. Nos 1-26. 2530 231; DG 2530 231.
Ohlssen. Nos 1-26. With the Barcarolle op 60. HQS 1338.
Larrocha. Nos 1-24. With the Berceuse op 57. SXL 6733.
Pollini. Nos 1-24. 2530 550.
Rondo in C minor op 1
Ludwik Stefanski. XL 0077.
Pouishnoff SAGA 5375.
Harasiewicz 6580 062.
Rondo a la Mazur op 5
Harasiewicz. 6580 062.
Ludwik Stefanski. XL 0077.
Rondo in E flat op 16
Horowitz. Recital 72969.
R Smith. Recital HQS 1290.
Ludwik Stefanski. XL 0077.
Rondo in C major for two pianos, op post
Halina Czerny-Stefanska, Ludwik Stefanski; (two pianos);
XL 0077.
Scherzi op 20, 31, 39, 54
V Ashkenazy. With Prelude op 45, Barcarolle op 60; SXL 6334.
Rubinstein. SB 2095. RCA LSC-2368.
Sonata op 4 in C minor
Maria Wilkomirska. XL 0081.
Sonata op 35 in B flat minor
V Ashkenazy SXL 6575; Lon 6794.
Rubinstein SB 2151; RCA LSC-3194.
Barenboim ASD 3064.

Sonata op 58 in B minor
  Lipatti. HQM 1163; ODYS 32160369.
  Rubinstein. SB 2151; RCA LSC-3194.
  Barenboim. ASD 3064.
Souvenir de Paganini op post
  Harasiewicz. Recital 6580 062.
  Barenboim. Recital ASD 3064.
Tarantelle op 43
  Rubinstein. Recital SB 6683.
  R Smith. Recital HQS 1290.
Variations brillantes op 12
  R Smith. Recital HQS 1290.
  Barbara Hesse-Bukowska. Recital XL 0079.
  Barenboim. Recital ASD 2963.
Variations on Marche des Puritains
  Harasiewicz. Recital 6580 062.
Waltzes 19
  Harasiewicz. Nos 1-19. 6580 003.
  Simon. Nos 1-19 TV 34580S; TURN 34580.
  Rubinstein. Nos 1-14. SB 6600; RCA LSC 2726.
  Lipatti. Nos 1-14. HLM 7075.

MISCELLANEOUS

*Largo in E flat; Funeral March in C minor; Cantabile in B flat;
Album leaf or Moderato in E major; Contredanse in G flat;
all op post*
  Halina Czerny-Stefanska. XL 0077.
*Fugue in A minor; Prelude in A flat; Swiss Boy variations or
Variations sur un air Allemand in E major; Hexameron vari-
ation; all op post*
  Barbara Hesse-Bukowska; XL 0079. (Other works that are
included on this and the previous record have been included
in the main list.)
  A selection of *Waltzes, Polonaises, Mazurkas* and *Preludes*
is played by Zbigniew Drzewiecki on the last Pleyel piano

Chopin had (Paris 1848), and which is now in Warsaw; on record no XL 0117.

VOCAL

Hulanka; Melodya; Moja Piesczotka; Narzecony; Niema Czego Trzeba; Spiew Grobowy; Wiosna (seven of Chopin's 19 songs)
   Tear, Ledger. Recital ZRG 814.

Index

No entries are included for the selected recordings of Chopin's music.

101

103

104

ML
410   Melville, Derek
C54   Chopin: ...
M47

DATE DUE			
DEC 16 '90			
FEB 1 '93			
NOV 1 '90			
DEC 06 '93			
MAY 22 '95			
JUN 05 '95			
MAY 15 '96			
DEC 08 1997			
AUG 12 '06			